ARCHERY

FROM A TO Z

ARCHERY
FROM A TO Z

An Introductory Guide
to a Sport Everyone Can Enjoy

CHRISTIAN BERG

STACKPOLE
BOOKS

Guilford, Connecticut

STACKPOLE BOOKS

Published by Stackpole Books
An imprint of The Rowman & Littlefield Publishing Group, Inc.
4501 Forbes Blvd., Ste. 200
Lanham, MD 20706
www.rowman.com

Distributed by NATIONAL BOOK NETWORK
800-462-6420

British Library Cataloguing in Publication Information available

Library of Congress Cataloging-in-Publication Data available

ISBN 978-0-8117-3834-7 (paperback)
ISBN 978-0-8117-6835-1 (e-book)

∞™ The paper used in this publication meets the minimum requirements of American National Standard for Information Sciences—Permanence of Paper for Printed Library Materials, ANSI/NISO Z39.48-1992.

Printed in the United States of America

CONTENTS

Acknowledgments   vi

Introduction   **Welcome to the Archery Family**   1

Chapter 1   **Evaluating Your Interest**   5

Chapter 2   **Bows and Basic Equipment**   13

Chapter 3   **What You Need to Know for Your First Bow**   41

Chapter 4   **Safety First**   55

Chapter 5   **Your First Shots**   63

Chapter 6   **Fine-tuning Your Stance**   85

Chapter 7   **More on Drawing and Anchoring**   91

Chapter 8   **Advanced Aiming**   101

Chapter 9   **Back Tension and the Surprise Release**   107

Chapter 10   **Why You Missed (and How to Fix It)**   119

Chapter 11   **Archery Games for Family Fun**   129

Chapter 12   **Introduction to Competitive Archery**   143

Index   159

ACKNOWLEDGMENTS

Although I have been a professional writer for nearly three decades—seventeen years as a daily newspaper reporter and the past decade as editor of *Petersen's Bowhunting* magazine—this is my first "real book," and I have many people to thank for helping make this dream a reality.

First, I'd like to thank former colleague David Blackwell for believing in the concept so strongly and nagging me until I finally finished the manuscript!

Second, I'd like to thank some of the many good people in the archery community who were so generous in making their time and expertise available throughout the process, particularly Rob Kaufhold, Heather Pfeil, and P. J. Reilly from Lancaster Archery Supply (lancasterarchery .com); John Dudley from Nock On Archery (nockonarchery.com); Brady Ellison from the US men's Olympic archery team (bradyellison.com); Levi Morgan from *Bow Life TV* (bowlife.com); and numerous staff members at the Archery Trade Association (archerytrade.org), USA Archery (teamusa .org/usa-archery), National Archery in Schools Program (naspschools .org), Scholastic 3-D Archery Association (s3da.org), Archery Shooters Association (asaarchery.com), National Field Archery Association (nfaausa .com), and International Bowhunting Organization (www.ibo.net).

Third, many thanks to photographer Jessica DeLorenzo for capturing such great images to illustrate this book, as well as publisher Judith Schnell and the production and design teams at Stackpole Books for giving me the opportunity to share my passion for archery with new shooters.

Last, but certainly not least, special thanks to my wife, Lindell, and sons, Toby and Timmy, for their endless love, support, and encouragement. Let's never stop chasing dreams together!

Welcome to the Archery Family

Archery is a perfect family sport because it can be enjoyed simultaneously by people of all ages, genders, and ability levels. The information contained in this book will provide you and your family with a solid foundation for your archery journey.

CONGRATULATIONS ON YOUR INTEREST IN BECOMING AN ARCHER! This book will guide you through the first steps of an exciting journey that can provide a lifetime of enjoyment.

Archery truly is a sport for everyone. You don't need to be fast, strong, tall, or good-looking to shoot a bow. And while a little athletic ability certainly won't hurt, you can become a successful shooter regardless of age,

Archery has played an important role in human history for thousands of years. This carved stone frieze from the ancient Egyptian city of Luxor depicts Pharaoh Ramses II firing his bow. SHUTTERSTOCK/BasPhoto

gender, or body type, making archery a perfect family activity that can be enjoyed simultaneously by several generations.

In addition to accommodating a wide range of participants, archery offers shooters a multitude of options for enjoying the sport. From simple backyard shooting, school programs, and local archery leagues to big-game hunting, professional tournament circuits, and international competitions such as the Olympics, the possibilities are virtually endless. Regardless of where your archery journey leads, the equipment knowledge and shooting fundamentals outlined here will provide a solid foundation and serve you well in future endeavors.

Becoming an archer will also make you a member of one of mankind's oldest fraternities. Archaeological records indicate that people have been wielding bows for at least 10,000 years, and archery's impact on human history has been profound. For prehistoric peoples, the invention of the bow dramatically increased the success of hunting efforts, ensuring a steady food supply that helped fuel future cultural advancements. The bow and arrow also quickly became a pivotal tool in the world of warfare, employed by all the great civilizations of antiquity, from Babylon and Egypt to Greece and Rome. And in the Middle Ages, many kingdoms rose and fell on the skills of well-trained bowmen.

Archery's popularity has gotten a huge boost from blockbuster Hollywood movies such as *The Hunger Games,* spawning a host of new shooters wielding copycat bows designed to look like those wielded by heroine Katniss Everdeen.
PHOTO COURTESY OF THE ARCHERY TRADE ASSOCIATION

Starting in the late 1500s, the advent of firearms slowly rendered bows and arrows technologically obsolete as hunting tools and weapons of war. Yet despite ever-advancing technology, archery has retained a loyal following through the centuries. The grace and fluid motions of the archer are undeniable, as are the magical qualities of an arrow in flight, which still captures the human imagination today as it did 10,000 years ago. A bow joins man (or woman) and machine in a unique way, and the excitement and satisfaction of a well-placed shot provide an unmistakable thrill.

Even in today's high-tech world of smartphones, self-driving automobiles, and robotic surgery, archery's popularity is as high as, if not higher than, ever. Recreational archery events and competitive tournaments routinely draw thousands of participants, and growing exposure of archery in popular culture is fueling a steady stream of new shooters. In recent years, for example, movie and TV characters such as Katniss Everdeen in *The Hunger Games*, Hawkeye in *The Avengers*, and Oliver Queen in *Arrow* have inspired countless young people to pick up a bow for the first time.

Others have been inspired by national pride and the success of shooters in international competition, such as the US men's team that captured Olympic silver at the 2016 Rio Games. Still others have caught the archery bug by watching television shows such as *Top Shot* or via countless online videos showing heart-pounding hunts, thrilling victories, and

Top-ranked US recurve archer Brady Ellison captured two medals at the 2016 Summer Olympics in Rio: a silver medal as part of the team competition and a bronze in the men's individual archery event. PHOTO COURTESY OF BRADY ELLISON

amazing trick shots. Despite its prehistoric roots, archery remains alive and well, with a very high "cool factor" in the twenty-first century.

Regardless of what has inspired you to become an archer or where the sport takes you, this guide will get you started the right way and have you hitting the bull's-eye in no time.

Welcome to the archery family. Let's get started!

CHAPTER 1
Evaluating Your Interest

Parental support is critical for young shooters, and participating in archery alongside your children will go a long way toward ensuring their long-term success.

WHEN BEGINNING A JOURNEY, IT IS HELPFUL TO KNOW THE DESTINATION or, at the very least, the direction you want to go. So, with that in mind, let's begin with a simple question: What do you want to do in archery? Your answer will help direct your initial steps on the path of the bow and arrow.

Think about what has attracted you to the sport and what you hope to accomplish. Maybe you've seen others shoot and want to find out what it feels like to draw a bow and launch your own arrows into flight. Maybe you are drawn to the history and romance of the sport and want to hone the hand-eye coordination required to wield a wooden longbow like Robin Hood. Maybe you have friends who bowhunt and want to join them as they pursue deer or elk. Or perhaps you are a fierce competitor with dreams of standing atop an Olympic podium with a gold medal around your neck as the American flag rises and the "Star Spangled Banner" plays.

Then again, it is entirely possible you have absolutely *no idea* what you want to do in archery, or that you are reading this book only because you are the parent of a child who has expressed interest in shooting. That is perfectly all right! However, for those parents using this guide as a reference in assisting children, I urge you to try archery yourself and consider shooting alongside your family. While there are many resources available to assist your children, nothing will aid their long-term success more than

YOUR LOCAL ARCHERY SHOP: AN INVALUABLE RESOURCE

As useful as this guide can be in helping you get started as an archer, there is no substitute for personal, one-on-one attention—and that's where your local archery shop comes in.

Archery dealers are a great resource for the latest and greatest bows, arrows, and archery gear, as well as technical expertise and shooting knowledge. Whether it's helping you choose the right bow, fixing an equipment problem, or answering questions about how to shoot your best, the staff at your local archery pro shop is invaluable. Many archery shops also offer indoor and/or outdoor shooting ranges, coaching clinics with certified instructors, and leagues where you can hone your shooting skills as you forge new friendships with fellow archers.

The Archery Trade Association has created a special website for new archers called Archery 360 (archery360.com) that includes a handy tool for finding archery dealers in your area. I encourage you to use it—and to make your local archery shop an integral part of your overall archery experience.

IMAGE COURTESY OF THE ARCHERY TRADE ASSOCIATION

your encouragement and support—and nothing is more likely to ensure that than developing your own passion for the sport.

Next, let's take a look at a few of today's most popular archery disciplines and the equipment generally associated with those pursuits. Whether you already have some solid ideas about your archery interests or you're still searching for direction, this information should help narrow your focus.

THREE AREAS OF FOCUS

As you'll soon discover when we cover archery equipment in chapter 2, the variety of bows available today can seem overwhelming. However, it really isn't that complicated. Heather Pfeil, program coordinator at Lancaster Archery Academy in Lancaster, Pennsylvania, helps introduce thousands of people to archery each year and said new shooters generally gravitate toward one of three main areas: recreational, Olympic recurve, or compound.

It could be argued that *all* bows are recreational, since shooting a bow for any purpose certainly is fun! However, "recreational archery" generally refers to entry-level gear not practically suited for use in serious archery competition or bowhunting. If you've ever shot a one-piece fiberglass longbow in gym class or pulled the string on a simple wooden recurve bow at summer camp, you've used recreational equipment. Although the cost of recreational bows tends to be quite modest, much of this equipment performs surprisingly well relative to the price; in recent years, archery manufacturers have offered a plethora of new recreational longbows, recurve bows, and even a few compound bows. Historically, the majority of recreational bows were geared toward young shooters, but today there are plenty of good adult models that will get you shooting for as little as $100. Recreational bows are a great way to try archery without breaking the bank, and they will certainly provide many hours of backyard shooting enjoyment. However, new shooters who progress quickly in the sport and want to tackle new challenges in competition or bowhunting may soon find themselves shopping for new equipment.

Many value-priced bows provide performance well beyond the price. The Galaxy Aspire, for example, costs less than $100 but offers a modern recurve design and all the accessory mounting options necessary to get started in Olympic-style target archery.
PHOTO COURTESY OF LANCASTER ARCHERY SUPPLY

Brady Ellison shoots his Hoyt recurve bow during the 2016 US Olympic trials.
PHOTO COURTESY OF BRADY ELLISON

Olympic-style recurve bows (also known as modern recurves) are designed specifically to produce top accuracy on the target range. Unlike the basic design of recreational equipment, today's top competition recurves are developed with the assistance of high-tech computer modeling programs and built using cutting-edge manufacturing processes. They are also outfitted with a host of accessories such as mechanical sights, arrow rests, and weighted stabilizers, all designed to help archers achieve maximum precision. The cost of an Olympic recurve is considerably higher than you would pay for recreational models, with average prices in the $400–$600 range and top models easily surpassing $1,000. However, these bows perform at a much higher level, offer the added benefit of personal customization, and will allow a new shooter to progress from basic shooting to local leagues to elite-level competition without having to purchase entirely new equipment.

Compound bows incorporate a mechanical system of cams and cables that allow shooters to store significantly more energy than they could with a longbow or recurve. As a result, compound bows have a substantial advantage when it comes to speed and power. Not surprisingly, the modern bowhunting scene is dominated by compound shooters. However,

Compound bows such as the one shown here employ a system of cams and cables that create a mechanical advantage, allowing shooters to store far more energy than they could with a longbow or recurve. PHOTO COURTESY OF JOHN DUDLEY/ NOCK ON ARCHERY

compounds are also widely used in competitions, from traditional bull's-eye targets to 3-D tournaments featuring life-size foam animal targets set along roving, wooded courses. Although there are a few entry-level compounds on the market, mainly geared toward young shooters, the price of compound bows is generally much higher than recreational bows, ranging from $300 on the low end to well over $1,000 for top models. However, like Olympic recurves, compound bows offer a great deal of

THE RIGHT TOOL FOR THE JOB

I Want To . . .	Common Bow Style
Shoot a bow like Robin Hood, Katniss Everdeen, Hawkeye, or Princess Merida	Traditional longbow or recurve
Shoot in the Olympics	Olympic-style recurve
Compete in field events with traditional bull's-eye targets	Olympic-style recurve or compound
Compete in roving 3-D shoots featuring life-size animal targets	Compound
Go bowhunting	Compound

versatility and customization options and allow shooters to venture into the realms of bowhunting and competition using the same equipment they use when shooting just for fun.

One additional bow genre that deserves mention includes high-end "traditional" longbows and recurves, wielded by a sizable contingent of bowhunters and target shooters who shoot instinctively (without the aid of mechanical bow sights or arrow rests)—much the same as human hunters and warriors have for thousands of years. Many of today's top bow manufacturers, such as Bear Archery and Martin Archery, continue to produce high-quality, hand-made, traditional longbows and recurves alongside their selection of high-tech compounds and Olympic recurves. Unlike recreational longbows and recurves, high-end longbows and recurves made using traditional craftsmanship are true works of art and carry price tags on par with top Olympic recurve and compound models.

SET YOUR GOALS

If you began this chapter with a fairly good idea of your archery interests, you've probably already started connecting the dots and refining your focus on a particular discipline or style of equipment. And if you started with a blank slate, hopefully something has piqued your interest.

Now is a good time to sit down and set some goals. Have individual family members think about their main areas of interest and what they would like to do. This could include short-term goals such as trying several different types of bows and long-term goals such as becoming a skilled enough archer to enter a tournament or try bowhunting. Of course it is possible—maybe even likely—that your goals will change along the way, but they are still valuable as a starting point.

Now let's take a more detailed look at the various bows and related gear you'll need to start shooting. Combined with your personal archery interests, this basic equipment knowledge will prepare you to head to the local archery dealer and shop for your first bow!

CHAPTER 2

Bows and Basic Equipment

THIS CHAPTER WILL GIVE YOU A SOLID UNDERSTANDING of each major bow type, how it works, and the basic accessories needed to shoot it. Each style of bow truly has its own "personality," so as we move through this chapter, think about how the style and capabilities of each bow type mesh with your own style and interests.

LONGBOW

The longbow—so named because of its length, typically about equal to the height of the shooter—dates back thousands of years but achieved legendary status in medieval England, where it was employed in battle with devastating efficiency against numerous enemies, most notably the French. English longbows were famous for their power, launching arrows capable of piercing the best armor of the day and pushing through oak up to 4 inches thick. The longbow was so crucial to England's military success that in the 1200s a law actually required all Englishmen to be equipped with a bow and arrows. In the 1300s another law required mandatory archery practice on Sunday and holidays—while outlawing all other sports!

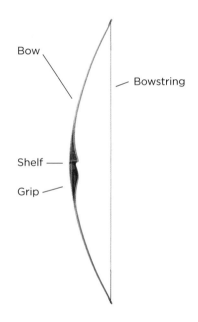

Parts of a longbow PHOTO COURTESY OF LANCASTER ARCHERY SUPPLY

Traditional longbows are made from a single piece of wood, often yew, elm, hickory, lemonwood, or Osage orange. Laminated models featuring various types of wood bonded together have also been developed, and a variety of contemporary longbows made from fiberglass and other synthetic materials are also available.

How a Longbow Works

A longbow is very simple, having no other parts except a string and a minimal handle, which often consists of nothing more than a piece of leather wrapped around the center of the bow on traditional models or a small piece of molded rubber on more contemporary versions. Longbows typically have little or no defined arrow rest, requiring shooters to use the top of their bow hand to support arrows while drawing and releasing. Longbows are drawn by hand and shot instinctively, which means aiming is done using simple hand-eye coordination. To shoot a longbow, the archer simply pulls the bowstring by hand, flexing the bow and storing energy in the limbs in the process. There is no set draw length, and the farther the string is drawn, the more the limbs are flexed and the more energy is stored. Upon release, the limbs return to their resting position, propelling the bowstring forward and transferring the stored energy to the arrow as it leaves the bow. When not in use, a longbow must be unstrung to release tension. Otherwise, the bow can take on a permanent flex, or "memory," of its strung position, reducing its ability to store energy.

Why Shoot a Longbow?

A longbow is a great choice for purists who want to connect with the history of archery and take on the challenge of learning to shoot instinctively. Longbows are simple to use, lightweight, and relatively inexpensive and require a minimal amount of associated gear.

What Are the Longbow's Limitations?

Although the longbow has a definite "cool factor" and will fit right in at the local Renaissance Fair, you will find relatively few shooters using them at your local archery league or tournament, where more modern equipment dominates. And while you can hunt with a longbow, it takes lots of practice to become proficient at even 20 yards, making it a short-range weapon. The longbow is also known for having a fairly stout

DID YOU KNOW?

During the Middle Ages, a skilled longbow archer could shoot ten to twelve arrows per minute, or one every 5 to 6 seconds. With a draw weight of 200 pounds, the English longbow was capable of launching arrows half a mile or more with enough force to knock a knight off his horse.

draw, forcing you to hold back a considerable amount of weight as you aim. Finally, although the longbow doesn't weigh much, its length can be unwieldy and make transporting it a challenge. In other words, it's not going to fit in the trunk of a compact car.

What Other Equipment Do I Need to Shoot a Longbow?

Other than some arrows, about the only thing you really need to shoot a longbow is a leather shooting glove or a shooting tab—a piece of leather that slips over your finger and is used to eliminate friction between your fingers and the bowstring.

TRADITIONAL RECURVE

Like the longbow, the history of the recurve bow dates back thousands of years. Originating in Asia, the recurve was used by many great civilizations, including the Persians, Chinese, Greeks, and Romans. The recurve bow gets its name because of the dual curvature of its limbs, which curve from the center of the bow inward toward the shooter before turning and flaring back out away from the shooter at the limb tips. So the limbs curve in and then curve out, or recurve.

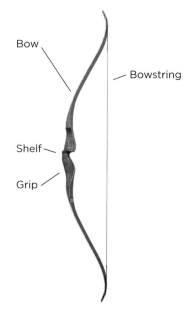

Parts of a traditional recurve bow
PHOTO COURTESY OF LANCASTER ARCHERY SUPPLY

A recurve bow design is able to generate significantly more energy than a longbow of the same length, resulting in greater power and more arrow speed. Because of this, it was possible to develop shorter bows that generated power equal to the much longer longbows. This made the recurve bow ideal for use in tight quarters or on horseback, where a longbow would be impractical.

Creating the shape of a recurve limb is difficult to do with a single material, so recurve limbs are typically made using a variety of materials. Historically, this involved the use of various types of wood with opposing grains, laminated together with animal resin to create the desired shape. More contemporary examples use a combination of wood, foam, and fiberglass.

How a Traditional Recurve Bow Works

Unlike a longbow, where the string contacts only the ends of the bow, the string on a recurve bow contacts much of the recurved portion of the limb end. When the string is drawn, the limbs flex more dramatically than a longbow's, resulting in increased energy storage. Like longbows, traditional recurve bows are drawn by hand and shot instinctively. However, recurves typically have a more defined grip area where the shooter holds the bow and an integrated arrow shelf where the arrow can rest as the bow is drawn and shot. Upon release, the limbs return to their resting position, propelling the bowstring forward and transferring the stored energy to the arrow as it leaves the bow. Like longbows, recurves have no set draw length and must be unstrung for storage to prevent the limbs from taking on additional flex and reducing their ability to store energy.

Why Shoot a Traditional Recurve?

Like longbows, traditional recurves are a great choice for those who want to connect with the history of archery at a relatively affordable price. Although hand drawn and shot instinctively, traditional recurves generally have a more defined grip to help shooters hold the bow properly and an integrated arrow shelf where the arrow can rest during the draw and release. Recurve bows are also faster and more powerful than longbows, as well as being more compact. They also tend to have a smoother feel to the draw because the draw weight of recurve limbs does not "stack," or increase, as quickly as on a longbow. Some traditional recurve models manufactured today also feature "take-down" designs that allow the limbs to be separated from the riser, further reducing the space required for storage or transport and creating the

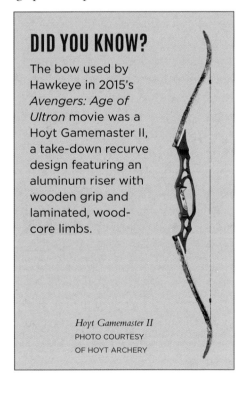

DID YOU KNOW?

The bow used by Hawkeye in 2015's *Avengers: Age of Ultron* movie was a Hoyt Gamemaster II, a take-down recurve design featuring an aluminum riser with wooden grip and laminated, wood-core limbs.

Hoyt Gamemaster II
PHOTO COURTESY
OF HOYT ARCHERY

ability to customize the bow by purchasing additional limb sets that will change the length and/or draw weight of the bow.

What Are a Traditional Recurve's Limitations?

It's probably obvious, but a traditional recurve won't let you experience the latest technological innovations in the archery world. Although you can hunt and participate in various competitions with a traditional recurve, those looking for maximum precision and customization would be better served with an Olympic-style recurve or compound bow.

What Other Equipment Do I Need to Shoot a Traditional Recurve?

Like the longbow, about the only thing you really need to shoot a traditional recurve is a leather shooting glove or a shooting tab. However, some contemporary models are designed to accommodate an arrow rest and/or bow sight, offering the opportunity to add a bit of modern flair.

OLYMPIC RECURVE

The jump from a traditional recurve to an Olympic, or modern, recurve is kind of like the jump from your grandmother's old rotary phone (remember those?) to the latest smartphone—there is simply no comparison when it comes to construction, capabilities, and the ability to customize. The Olympic recurve gets its name because it is the *only* style of bow used in the Olympics. However, this style of bow is widely used by hundreds of thousands of shooters around the world, most of whom are not world-class competitors.

The riser—the center portion of the bow containing the handle, limb pockets, and accessory mounting holes—on an Olympic recurve is typically made from metal such as aluminum or magnesium, although some high-end models are made of carbon fiber and some entry-level risers are molded from synthetic materials such as nylon. Olympic recurve limbs are typically made with a combination of laminated materials such as carbon, synthetic foam, and fiberglass. The limbs are designed using advanced computer modeling software that allows engineers to customize flex for precise energy loading and an elongated "sweet spot" at full draw, making the bows feel smoother and more comfortable to hold while aiming.

All Olympic recurves feature a take-down design that allows you to easily remove the limbs from the riser. This not only makes these bows easy to transport but allows for a great deal of customization, since additional limb sets can be purchased to change the draw weight and/or

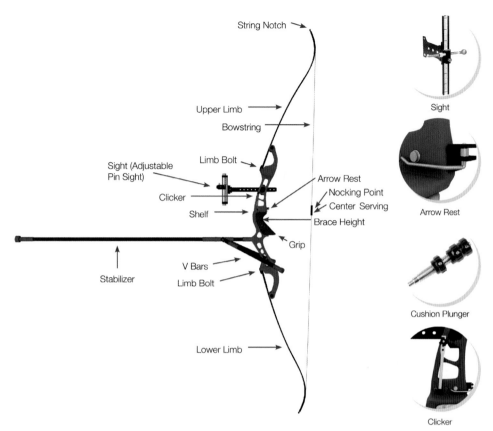

Parts of an Olympic recurve bow ILLUSTRATION COURTESY OF USA ARCHERY

overall length of the bow. Most Olympic recurve risers also incorporate the International Limb Fitting (ILF) system, a universal pocket design that allows you to use ILF limbs from any manufacturer regardless of the brand of your riser. A take-down design with the ILF system allows an Olympic recurve bow to "grow" with an archer, since additional draw weight and bow length can be added as the shooter grows. This versatility also allows new shooters to save money, since they can purchase a quality riser and inexpensive limbs as they start out. Later, if they need more draw weight or become more serious about competition, they can simply purchase longer, stronger, or higher-quality limbs without replacing the entire bow and related gear.

How an Olympic Recurve Bow Works

Like traditional recurves, Olympic recurves are hand drawn and have no set draw length. However, instead of shooting instinctively, the archer uses a riser-mounted bow sight for aiming. And instead of shooting the arrow off a shelf integrated in the riser, Olympic recurves use mechanical arrow rests that guide the arrow on its way. Upon release, energy stored in the limbs is transferred to the arrow as it leaves the bow. And, like traditional recurves, an Olympic recurve must be unstrung when not in use to prevent limb damage.

Why Shoot an Olympic Recurve?

The Olympic recurve is a great choice for anyone who wants to participate in archery competition. It is also an excellent option for those who want to combine the relatively simple mechanics of a recurve design with the added aiming precision of a mechanical sight and the increased accuracy afforded by a mechanical arrow rest. In many ways, the Olympic recurve is a perfect blend of archery's past and present.

What Are an Olympic Recurve's Limitations?

Because it is designed for target competition, an Olympic recurve is not practically suited for bowhunting and is not the best option for those more interested in roving, outdoor competitions such as those featuring 3-D foam animal targets.

What Other Equipment Do I Need to Shoot an Olympic recurve?

As mentioned, Olympic recurves are outfitted with mechanical bow sights and arrow rests. Other accessories typically found on Olympic recurves include long, weighted stabilizers to help shooters steady their aim and a clicker to ensure consistent draw length. You'll also need a shooting tab. We'll discuss these more in a bit.

COMPOUND BOW

Invented just fifty years ago, the compound bow is the new kid on the archery block. However, its unsurpassed speed, incredible precision, and a host of high-tech features have made it a force to be reckoned with. In fact, in just five decades, compound bow technology has gone from something ridiculed as a passing fad to something that has literally revolutionized the sport. To help you understand why this is the case, consider this: A "fast" Olympic recurve bow shoots arrows between 200 and 220 feet per second, while the fastest compound bows can fling arrows down range at speeds of 350 feet per second or more—a 75 percent speed advantage! If you have a serious "need for speed," a compound bow is the obvious choice.

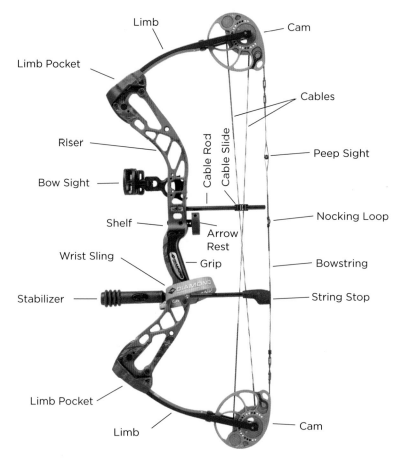

Parts of a compound bow PHOTO COURTESY OF DIAMOND ARCHERY

Today's compound bows typically feature a riser made from aluminum or carbon, along with short, stiff, fiberglass limbs that sometimes incorporate other materials such as carbon fiber. Compound bows are generally drawn and shot using a mechanical release aid that has a small, trigger-activated caliper that holds the string during the draw and then opens to release the string. Release aids can either be held in the shooter's hand or strapped around the wrist. Release aids ensure a consistent, smooth string release for maximum accuracy. And because most compound bows are quite short relative to longbows and recurves, the string angle is quite severe and leaves little room for fingers at full draw.

How a Compound Bow Works

Compound bows create mechanical advantages for shooters by incorporating a cam system and cable or cables that work in tandem with the bowstring. Although there are numerous types of cam systems—single cams, dual cams, and hybrid or binary cams—they all essentially serve as a pulley system that creates a leverage advantage and enables archers to store additional energy in the bow. In simple terms, when you pull string out of a compound bow during the draw cycle, the cam or cams rotate and take up cable at the same time, drawing the limbs together and storing energy as they compress. Because of the oval shape of the cam or cams, the weight required to draw the string increases steadily until it reaches a peak just before the cam or cams rotate to the back side, at which time the shooter gains a leverage advantage that greatly reduces the amount of force required to draw the bowstring the rest of the way back. This leverage advantage is called "let-off," and many modern compound bow designs create let-off up to 85 percent. That means if the bow has a peak draw weight of 60 pounds, the amount of force required to hold the bowstring back at full draw will be just 9 pounds. Compound bows also have defined draw lengths set to match the shooter. When the preset draw length is reached, posts mounted on the cam or cams contact the cables or limbs and force the bowstring to stop. The back end of the draw is referred to as "the wall," since the string cannot be pulled back any farther.

Shooters experience two big practical advantages as a result of a compound bow design. First, because the draw cycle of a compound bow only requires the shooter to pull the bow's peak weight for a short period of time, compound shooters are able to store significantly more energy in their bows compared to a longbow or recurve. This additional energy translates into faster arrow speeds and a flatter arrow trajectory. Second, because the let-off created by a compound system makes it very easy to hold the string at full draw, compound shooters can take their time and aim very precisely prior to releasing the arrow. In hunting situations, this allows archers to wait for an animal to present the proper shooting angle before releasing the arrow; in competition, it allows archers to concentrate and wait until their form is perfect and aim is dead on before releasing the arrow. Thanks to the unique advantages offered by the compound bow design, most archers are able to shoot a compound bow far more accurately than a longbow or recurve.

Why Shoot a Compound Bow?

If your archery interests revolve around outdoor adventure, the compound bow is your obvious choice. Compound bows are, by far, the dominant style of bow used for hunting and 3-D competitions featuring life-size foam animal targets set along roving, wooded courses. Compound bows are also the dominant type of bow used in US field archery events, which feature both outdoor and indoor competitions using both conventional bull's-eye targets and two-dimensional animal targets. Compound bows are also a great choice for shooters who love technology, as compound models are on the cutting edge of bow design.

WHAT ARE A COMPOUND BOW'S LIMITATIONS?

Because they are so mechanical, a compound bow is not the best choice for someone more interested in the history of archery. The multiple moving parts also create more potential for failure and require more maintenance than recurve bows. Further, doing things such as changing a bowstring or adjusting the draw-length setting on a compound bow often requires specialized equipment such as a bow press, necessitating a visit to the local archery shop.

What Other Equipment Do I Need to Shoot a Compound bow?

Like an Olympic recurve, a compound bow uses a mechanical bow sight and arrow rest. You'll also need a mechanical release aid, along with other accessories such as a peep sight, wrist sling, nock set or nocking loop, and perhaps some optional accessories such as vibration dampeners and a stabilizer. We'll cover all those items later in the chapter.

ARROWS

Regardless of what kind of bow you shoot, you're going to need arrows. Let's go over the basics.

Nock   Fletching/Vanes   Shaft   Fieldpoint

Parts of an arrow PHOTO COURTESY OF BLACK EAGLE ARROWS

WHAT ARROW SIZE DO I NEED?

As you look at various types of arrows, you'll probably notice that different shafts are labeled with different numbers, such as 2114, 1813, 1000, 750, 570, or 340. These numbers refer to the arrow size. Different arrow manufacturers use different number systems for arrow sizes, so it can be confusing. In simple terms, however, arrow size simply refers to the stiffness and weight of the arrow. Bows with high draw weights require arrows with more stiffness (called arrow "spine") and weight than bows with lower draw weights. So an arrow that works well on a bow shot by a grown man would not be the right choice for use with a youth bow.

While it can seem complicated, it's actually pretty easy! Your local archery dealer is a great resource to help you choose an arrow, and each arrow manufacturer has a shaft selection chart that will tell you which size is right for your bow, based on your draw length and draw weight.

Arrows come in many different varieties, depending on the application. Your local archery pro shop is a great resource for selecting the right arrows for your shooting style.

The main part of the arrow is called the shaft. Historically, arrow shafts were made from solid wood cylinders, but nowadays you basically have two choices when it comes to shafts: aluminum or carbon fiber tubes. Carbon arrows have surged in popularity over the past twenty years because they do not permanently bend and are very durable.

At the back end of the arrow shaft is the nock, which attaches to the bowstring. Nocks are typically made of plastic and can be either glued onto the end of the arrow or fit inside the rear of the shaft.

Also at the back end of the shaft is the fletching—miniature wings that help stabilize the arrow in flight. Arrows used for longbows and traditional recurves typically use natural feather fletching because feathers easily flex out of the way as the arrow slides against the bow when shot. Arrows used for Olympic recurve bows and compounds, however, typically use plastic fletching called vanes. Plastic vanes are more durable and weather resistant than feathers and can be precision molded in a variety of shapes and sizes to provide very consistent arrow flight.

At the front end of the arrow is the point. Like nocks, points can be either glued into the front of the arrow shaft directly or screwed into threaded inserts that are glued into the front of the shaft. Arrows with inserts allow you to use different types of points on the same arrow. For example, bowhunters typically screw a rounded fieldpoint on the shaft for practice and replace it with a razor-sharp broadhead for hunting.

As with other types of archery gear, there are lots of choices when it comes to choosing what arrows to shoot. However, for new shooters I highly recommend sticking with a basic carbon or aluminum shaft that is moderately priced. The truth of the matter is, you are quite likely to break and/or lose some arrows as you learn the sport, and there really is no need to spend a lot of money on arrows right now. You'll probably need more arrows before long anyhow, and you can always upgrade later as you advance in the sport.

BOW ACCESSORIES AND RELATED GEAR

Let's take a look at some basic bow accessories and other archery gear. How many of these items you actually need will depend on the type of bow you ultimately choose to shoot.

Also keep in mind that there are literally thousands of archery products on the market, with more being developed all the time. The following is by no means an exhaustive list of equipment, but it does cover the essentials, along with some useful "nice to have" items you might find helpful as you begin your archery journey.

Bow Sight

A bow sight is mounted to the bow's riser and simply provides a reference point that tells you where to hold your bow at full draw to hit a certain spot downrange. Bow sights come in many styles for both recurve and compound bows and are typically targeted either for competition or hunting use. Competition sights usually offer a single aiming point that can be adjusted for various ranges, while hunting sights typically offer multiple aiming points that can be preset for various distances, allowing archers to take advantage of quick opportunities in the field without having to make a sight adjustment.

From top, these are examples of bow sights for Olympic-style recurve bows, target compound bows, and hunting compound bows. TOP PHOTO COURTESY OF AXCEL; MIDDLE PHOTO COURTESY OF SPOT-HOGG ARCHERY; BOTTOM PHOTO COURTESY OF TRUGLO

Regardless of model, the basic concept remains the same. Bow sights allow for windage (left/right) and elevation (up/down) adjustments that change the location of the aiming reference to correspond with the arrow's impact point. Once the sight is properly calibrated for the bow, the shooter simply places the appropriate reference point (aiming pin) on target and uses it to continue aiming as the arrow is released. Many competition shooters also have a magnified scope that allows them to better see the target from far away and increase aiming precision.

Peep Sight

A peep sight is a small, round aperture of metal or plastic that is mounted in the bowstring above the arrow and used in tandem with the bow sight as part of an overall aiming system. When the bow is drawn, the archer aligns the string so that he or she can look through the peep sight and then align the proper reference point on the sight with the target. In practice, a peep sight serves as a rear reference point and the bow sight serves

A peep sight is mounted within the bowstring and serves as a rear reference point that is aligned with the bow sight in front.

as a front reference point for proper aiming alignment, much like the rear and front iron sights on a rifle. Peep sights are most commonly used on compound bows but are also found on some recurve bows.

Kisser Button

Like a peep sight, a kisser button provides a rear reference point for proper aiming alignment. A kisser button is a small, rubber disc mounted to the bowstring at the location where the string meets the corner of the shooter's mouth at full draw. By placing the kisser button against the lips in the same spot shot after shot, the shooter is able to achieve consistent sight alignment.

A kisser button helps achieve consistent aiming by allowing the shooter to place the button in the corner of the mouth on each shot.

Arrow Rest

Although arrow rests are used on some traditional bows, they are most commonly found on Olympic recurves and compounds. An arrow rest supports the arrow as the bow is drawn and provides critical guidance during the first instant of the shot as the string propels the arrow from the bow. Arrow rests also prevent the arrow shaft and vanes from contacting the bow riser, which can cause erratic arrow flight.

As with bow sights, arrow rests are generally customized for either target shooting or bowhunting. Target rests feature designs that create minimal contact with the arrow and help smooth out the arrow's initial several inches of travel. Hunting rests, meanwhile, focus more on securely containing the arrow while stalking through the woods and/or shooting at odd angles, where the arrow might completely fall off a target rest.

Arrow rests are typically customized for either target shooting (top) or bowhunting (bottom). TOP PHOTO COURTESY OF FUSE ARCHERY; BOTTOM PHOTO COURTESY OF TRUGLO

Nock Set

A nock set is a small brass ring crimped onto the bowstring just above where the arrow is nocked. A nock set ensures that the arrow is placed on the string in exactly the same spot for each shot.

A nock set is crimped onto the bowstring to ensure that the arrow is placed in exactly the same spot on every shot. CHRISTIAN BERG PHOTO

Nocking Loop

A nocking loop serves the same purpose as a nock set. However, it is a loop tied onto the bowstring above and below the arrow nock. A mechanical release aid is then attached to the loop and the drawstring is pulled via the nocking loop.

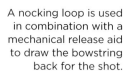 A nocking loop is used in combination with a mechanical release aid to draw the bowstring back for the shot.

Stabilizer

Stabilizers are used on both Olympic recurve and compound bows. As the name implies, a stabilizer is a weighted rod designed to help the shooter hold steady on target by reducing bow movement at full draw. Stabilizers also incorporate materials that help absorb vibration created by the shot. Reduced vibration means less shot noise and less bow movement in the shooter's hand as the arrow leaves the bow, enhancing accuracy.

Stabilizers are weighted rods designed to help archers hold the bow steadier at full draw. Stabilizers designed for target shooting (top) tend to be longer to get the weight farther away from the bow; stabilizers designed for hunting (bottom) tend to be smaller and lighter to allow for added maneuverability in the field. PHOTOS COURTESY OF BEE STINGER

Stabilizers attach to the bow via a mounting hole on the lower end of the riser. Stabilizers for target shooters can be several feet long and sometimes incorporate rear-facing weights to further enhance bow balance. Stabilizers for hunting bows tend to be much smaller and lighter—sometimes as short as a few inches and weighing just several ounces—to allow for maximum maneuverability in the field.

Bow Sling

Used on Olympic recurve and compound bows, a bow sling helps prevent accidentally dropping the bow after releasing an arrow. Compound shooters generally use wrist slings, while recurve shooters generally use finger slings, though both serve the same purpose.

A wrist sling (top) used on a compound bow or a finger sling (bottom) used on an Olympic recurve both prevent the bows from being accidentally dropped while in use. TOP PHOTO COURTESY OF TRUGLO

Shooting Gloves

Leather shooting gloves are commonly used by those shooting longbows and traditional recurve bows. Designed to be worn on the release hand (the one that draws and releases the bowstring), they come in a variety of configurations, from full gloves to skeletal three-finger designs that protect the index, middle, and ring fingers from friction.

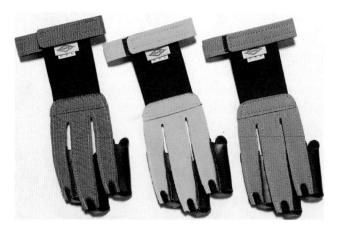

Shooting gloves help protect the archer's fingers from friction with the bowstring.
PHOTO COURTESY OF NEET PRODUCTS

Shooting Tabs

Like shooting gloves, shooting tabs are used by those who shoot longbows or traditional recurves. Tabs are also the most common method of release for Olympic recurve shooters. Like shooting gloves, tabs protect the fingers of the release hand from friction and also help ensure a smoother release. Basic shooting tabs are nothing more than leather pieces with a finger hole. Many tabs also include a layer of real or synthetic animal

Like a shooting glove, a shooting tab is designed to eliminated friction between the archer's fingers and bowstring, while also providing for a smoother release.
PHOTO COURTESY OF NEET PRODUCTS

fur to further reduce friction, along with a small plastic spacer to aid in proper finger positioning. Tabs used by Olympic recurve shooters generally incorporate an aluminum frame with built-in anchor point references and adjustable thumb and finger placement settings that allows shooters to customize the feel for their particular shooting style.

Release Aid

While longbows and recurves are generally fired using a shooting glove or tab, compound bows are generally shot via a mechanical release aid that incorporates a metal jaw or hook that holds the string while the bow is drawn and aimed. On most releases, the bow is fired via an integrated trigger system that causes the jaw or hook to open and release the string. However, many competition shooters use release aids activated simply by increasing tension on the string. We'll discuss more about how to use back-tension release aids as a training aid in chapter 9. Mechanical release aids come in a variety of styles, though the two most common are wrist-strap release aids with index-finger triggers and handheld release aids with thumb-activated triggers.

The two most common styles of release aids used by compound bow shooters are wrist-strap, index-finger releases (top right) and handheld, thumb-activated releases (bottom left). LEFT PHOTO COURTESY OF TRU-FIRE; RIGHT PHOTO COURTESY OF TRUGLO

Clicker

A clicker is a simple device, usually made of spring steel, that mounts to the riser and makes an audible click when the shooter's exact draw length has been reached. Clickers are most commonly used on Olympic recurve bows to keep shooters from varying the length of their draw from shot to shot. However, clickers are sometimes used on target-oriented compound bows.

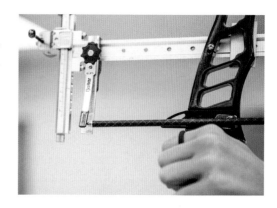

A clicker is a piece of spring steel that makes an audible click when the arrow is drawn to a set point. This helps recurve shooters maintain a consistent draw length from shot to shot.

Bow Stringer

Used on longbows and recurves, a bow stringer allows you to gain the necessary leverage to place the bowstring on the limbs before shooting and remove it after shooting. A bow stringer generally consists of a rope and fittings for each limb that allow the shooter to safely create enough limb flex to string and unstring the bow with minimal effort.

A bow stringer helps gain the needed leverage to string and unstring a longbow or recurve.

Quiver

No matter what kind of bow you shoot, you'll need a quiver to hold your arrows. By far the most common style of quiver used today is the hip quiver, which is simply worn around the waist on a belt. Many hip quivers not only hold arrows but also incorporate extra pockets and attachment loops to store shooting tabs, release aids, arrow pullers, binoculars, and related gear. On hunting bows, quivers mounted directly to the bow are very popular because they hold arrows securely and quietly, keep them at the ready, and incorporate a protective shield to prevent accidental contact with razor-sharp broadheads.

Hip quivers (top left) are very popular with recreational and target archers, while bowhunters generally prefer bow-mounted quivers (right). TOP LEFT PHOTO COURTESY OF NEET PRODUCTS; BOTTOM RIGHT PHOTO COURTESY OF TRUGLO

Bow Stands

Although they aren't required to shoot, a bow stand is a handy item most archers will appreciate. Designed to hold the bow upright and off the ground when not in use, bow stands come in a variety of models for both recurve and compound bows and are extremely useful on the practice range, in competition, or simply when you're outside shooting for fun.

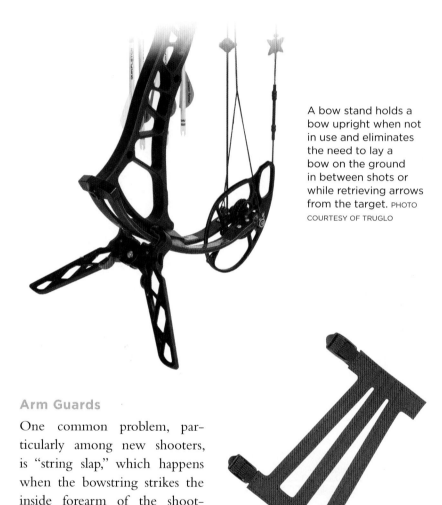

A bow stand holds a bow upright when not in use and eliminates the need to lay a bow on the ground in between shots or while retrieving arrows from the target. PHOTO COURTESY OF TRUGLO

Arm Guards

One common problem, particularly among new shooters, is "string slap," which happens when the bowstring strikes the inside forearm of the shooter's bow arm after the arrow is released. Using an arm guard—typically made from leather, plastic, or padded fabric—will protect your arm from the pain.

An arm guard protects the archer's forearm from accidental contact with the bowstring while shooting. PHOTO COURTESY OF NEET PRODUCTS

Chest Protectors

Commonly used by longbow and recurve shooters, these sling-style devices are worn over the shoulder of the drawing arm. As the name implies, they protect the chest from contact with the string, particularly for female shooters. They also help keep clothing out of the string's path, avoiding contact that could result in errant shots. Chest protectors are typically not used by compound bow shooters, since compounds are shorter and have more severe string angles that eliminate chest contact.

Chest protectors prevent accidental contact between the chest and bowstring while shooting and also help keep loose clothing out of the string's path.

Binoculars

You might think of binoculars as something more appropriate for birders than archers. However, seeing exactly where your arrow hit the target can be tricky, even at 20 yards. Binoculars make checking your accuracy a lot easier and will save lots of walking back and forth between your bow and the target.

Binoculars are a handy tool on the shooting range, allowing you to see exactly where your arrows hit without having to constantly walk back and forth from the shooting line to the target.

Laser Rangefinder

A laser rangefinder is certainly not a necessity for a new shooter. However, it is an extremely handy tool that will instantly tell you the exact distance to your target—and not knowing that distance is probably the number-one cause of missed shots. Simply point the rangefinder at the spot you want to range, press the button, and the unit will bounce a laser beam off the object and tell

A laser rangefinder is a very handy tool that eliminates the need to guess the distance to your target. Knowing the exact range will greatly help you know where to aim for an accurate shot.
PHOTO COURTESY OF HALO OPTICS

you the distance in yards or meters. Many units also automatically compensate for angled shots and let you know exactly what distance to "aim for," regardless of the actual linear distance.

TARGETS

The final equipment category we need to look at is targets. Simply put, you can't shoot your bow without one; and unless you want to drive to the local pro shop or archery club every time you want to shoot your bow, you're going to need a target of your own.

Archery targets come in a variety of shapes, sizes, and materials, from ultra-portable targets that can be thrown in the backseat of your car to extra-large targets such as life-size elk and bison. Prices vary accordingly, but in general you can expect to spend anywhere from $80 to $150 for a quality portable target that will accommodate your backyard shooting sessions.

There are three main types of targets available, each with its own pros and cons. Let's discuss them briefly.

Bag Targets

As the name implies, a bag-style target consists of a bag stuffed with dense fibers or other material that absorbs the arrow's impact. The exterior bag is typically made of fabric or woven plastic mesh with a bull's-eye target printed on it. Sometimes the opposite side of the bag will have secondary aiming spots or an archery game board. Bag targets tend to be reasonably priced and are very easy to transport. Many models also have grommets on the top corners that make these targets easy to hang in an elevated position. Bag targets also allow for very easy arrow removal. However,

Bag targets such as the Delta Wedgie are inexpensive and easy to transport and allow easy arrow removal. PHOTO COURTESY OF DMT TARGETS

bag targets aren't generally as durable as other styles and cannot be used with hunting broadheads, which will shred the outer bag.

Solid Foam Targets

Solid foam targets are the most durable, weather-resistant style. They will stand up to thousands of shots from both practice points and broadheads and will last several seasons, even outdoors. They come in a variety of shapes and sizes, from simple foam cubes with aiming points painted on the exterior to life-size animals.

Because of their solid, dense foam, these targets are relatively heavy compared with other styles, and removing arrows deeply embedded in the foam can sometimes be difficult. Solid foam targets also generally run on the higher end of the price spectrum.

Solid foam targets such as the Rinehart Pyramid are extremely durable and can be shot with both practice points and broadheads. PHOTO COURTESY OF RINEHART TARGETS

Layered Foam Targets

Layered foam targets are constructed by vertically stacking many thin layers of foam sheeting and then tightly compressing the layers using bands or heat welding. When an arrow strikes the target, it slides between two of the compressed foam layers and is stopped via friction.

In many ways, a layered foam target offers a nice middle ground between bag targets and solid foam targets in terms of weight, durability, and price. Arrow removal from layered foam targets is quite easy compared to solid foam targets but harder than bag targets. And you can shoot both practice points and broadheads into them, though they will generally not take as many shots as a solid foam target before wearing out.

Layered foam targets such as the Delta Mo' Foam CHUNK combine many of the benefits of a bag target, such as easy arrow removable and portability, while also standing up to shots using both practice points and broadheads. PHOTO COURTESY OF DMT TARGETS

LET'S GO SHOPPING!

Whew! This was a long chapter. There was an awful lot of material to digest, and you should be proud of yourself for sticking with it to the end. You now have a basic understanding of each major style of bow, bow accessories, arrows, and other basic archery gear. Now it's time to head to the local archery dealer and get a bow of your own. In the next chapter we'll cover some important things to consider as you review your options.

CHAPTER 3

What You Need to Know for Your First Bow

A visit to your local archery pro shop should be your first step in the bow-buying process. Try out a variety of bow styles, and figure out which suits you best.

GETTING YOUR FIRST BOW IS A BIG EVENT! And now that you've learned about your options and the basic equipment involved, you're ready to dive in and make a very exciting purchase.

The information in this chapter is designed to help find the right bow for *you*. Remember, there are a lot of great bows out there in all styles and price ranges, but only you can decide exactly which one makes the most sense for your particular interests and budget.

EYE DOMINANCE

One of the first things your archery dealer will do is test your eye dominance to determine whether you need a right- or left-handed bow. If you're planning to purchase a bow via mail order or someplace other than an established archery dealer, it is extremely important to do this for yourself.

Every person has a dominant eye that takes precedence over the other in the way the brain processes visual information. To shoot your best, it is critical to aim with your dominant eye. Surprisingly, whether you write or throw with your right or left hand is not always a reliable indicator of eye dominance, which is why you should go through this simple exercise to check.

First, stand with your arms extended in front of your body. Now move your hands together and form a triangular peep hole by bringing your thumbs and index fingers together as pictured.

Next, look through the hole between your hands and focus on a nearby object. Slowly bring your hands back to your face as you continue to focus on the object. Your hands should naturally come back to your dominant eye, which will allow you to complete the exercise without ever losing sight of the object. If you repeat the process and bring your hands back to your non-dominant eye, you should notice that the object becomes blocked by the back of your hand as it nears your face.

If you are right-eye dominant, you'll shoot a right-handed bow. And if you are left-eye dominant, you will shoot a left-handed bow. It's as simple as that.

TRY BEFORE YOU BUY

By now you've learned enough to have a pretty good idea what style of bow fits your personality, whether that's a traditional longbow or recurve, an Olympic recurve, or a compound. However, if you are brand new to archery and relatively unfamiliar with equipment, I *strongly encourage* you to begin the buying process by visiting your local archery dealer and shooting as many styles of bows as possible. Even if you are dead set on a particular style of bow, it would be a shame to rush into your purchase without at least experiencing what it feels like to shoot the other styles. If you've never done this before, I guarantee you will be surprised by just how different the shooting experiences are, and this exercise will either reinforce your previous thoughts or prompt you to consider other directions. Besides, trying different bows is fun, and employees at any reputable pro shop will be more than happy to help. After all, their job is to help you find just the right bow, and the only way to do that is to shoot them!

DRAW LENGTH

The next thing your archery dealer is likely to do is figure out your draw length. Draw length is the actual distance you pull the bowstring back from its resting position to where you release the arrow. Draw length is typically measured in inches and rounded to the nearest half inch. Each

Many archery shops have a special bow customers can draw to instantly determine their proper draw length.

person has an optimal draw length, and that is directly related to your body size. For young shooters, optimal draw length will increase as they grow, but for fully grown adult shooters, optimal draw length is constant once determined.

There are a couple ways to determine your optimal draw length. Perhaps the easiest is by using a special draw-length test bow often found at archery pro shops. These bows feature an arrow with measurement marks that is permanently attached to the bow. A draw-length reading can be taken simply by having a customer hold the bow and draw the arrow back to the aiming position.

If you need to determine your draw length on your own, an alternate method is to get a tape measure and have someone measure your wingspan from the tip of one middle finger to the tip of the other middle while you stand upright with your arms spread out to your sides. A general rule of thumb is to divide your wingspan by 2.5 as a starting point for your draw length.

Interestingly, although each archer has an optimal draw length based on his or her body size, not all bows have set draw lengths. Longbows and recurves have no set draw length, and it is possible to shoot them at a variety of draw lengths. For example, a youth with a 20-inch draw length, a woman with a 25-inch draw length, and a man with a 30-inch draw length could all shoot the same recurve bow simply by pulling the string to their draw length and releasing the arrow.

Virtually all compound bows have a defined draw length that is mechanically set for each individual archer via the cam system. Once set at a particular draw length, a compound bow is designed only to be shot at that exact draw length unless it is manually adjusted. For example, I have a 29-inch draw length. When drawing my compound bow, I would never stop at 27 inches and release an arrow, because the bow is designed to be brought back to full draw (where the let-off occurs) and held there while aiming. Similarly, I cannot draw the bow past 29 inches, because once a compound bow reaches full draw, posts mounted on the cams contact the cables and/or limbs and physically prevent the bowstring from being pulled back any farther. (**Note:** Some compound designs are an exception to this rule, but we'll discuss that later in this chapter.) Most compound models will also accommodate only a certain range of draw lengths, such as 25–30 inches, for example. If you are shopping for a compound bow, it's important to know your draw length and then find a bow that can be adjusted to fit you properly.

THE COOL FACTOR

Finding a bow that fits you is critical to a successful and enjoyable archery experience. But let's face it; what we all want—whether we are young or just young at heart—is a bow that's cool! Fortunately, there are a lot of really cool bows out there, and manufacturers have really stepped up their game in recent years when it comes to designing equipment that is not only highly functional but also extremely stylish.

From traditional bows designed to capture the iconic look seen in such movies as *The Hunger Games* series to flashy compounds with fluorescent colors and trendy patterns, today's bows look as good as they shoot. And while having a tricked-out bow that turns heads at the local range may not help you put more arrows in the bull's-eye, it will make shooting your bow more fun. And isn't that what it's really all about?

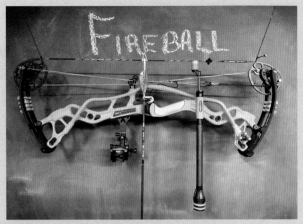

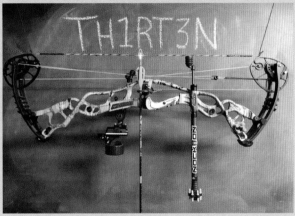

Today's archery equipment manufacturers pay a lot of attention to aesthetics, offering bows and related accessories in a variety of popular color schemes that make the bows look as good as they shoot. JOHN DUDLEY/NOCK ON ARCHERY PHOTOS

DRAW WEIGHT

Draw weight is the amount of force, measured in pounds, required to pull the bowstring from its resting position to full draw. As with draw length, your optimal draw weight will vary based on your body type. Simply put, the stronger you are, the more draw weight you will be able to handle. And the more draw weight you pull, the more energy you will store in your bow and the faster your arrows will travel.

Although more draw weight does equal more energy and arrow speed, it is important to stress here that your goal should *not* be to draw as much weight as you can physically handle. Rather, the goal is to find a *comfortable* draw weight that allows you to draw and shoot your bow repeatedly without struggling and while maintaining proper form shot after shot. Archers who attempt to shoot more draw weight than they can adequately handle are said to be "over bowed." This is a recipe for injury and a host of bad shooting habits that will result in poor accuracy. **DO NOT** give in to the temptation to pull more bow weight than you can handle. It will only lead to frustration. We'll discuss some general guidelines on draw weights in a bit, but as you try various bows during your selection process, it's a good idea to experiment with a variety of draw weights so that you can feel the difference and find a poundage that makes sense for you.

On longbows and recurves, draw weight is directly related to draw length—the amount of weight required to draw the bowstring increases steadily as it is pulled and the amount of flex in the limbs increases. Because longbows and recurves do not have set draw lengths, the industry has adopted a standard of rating longbow and recurve limbs based on their holding weight at 28 inches of draw. For example, a 45-pound

EXAMPLE DRAW WEIGHTS OF A 40-POUND RECURVE BOW

Draw Length	Draw Weight
24 in.	33 lb.
25 in.	35 lb.
26 in.	37 lb.
27 in.	38 lb.
28 in.	40 lb.
29 in.	42 lb.
30 in.	44 lb.

longbow or recurve means that when the bowstring is drawn to a length of 28 inches, it will require 45 pounds of force to get it there—and the shooter will have to continue holding the entire 45 pounds of pressure while aiming. However, the same bow may have a draw weight of just 30 pounds at 25 inches of draw length and a hefty 60 pounds at 31 inches of draw length. This steady increase in pressure as string travel increases is commonly referred to among archers as "stacking."

If you are in the market for a longbow or recurve bow, your archery dealer will help you select a bow that will generate a proper draw weight for you, based on your draw length. Generally speaking, it is a good idea to err on the "light" side, and many new adult shooters start out with draw weights as little as 15 to 20 pounds.

On compound bows, there is still a relationship between draw length and draw weight, but it is not so direct. That's because, thanks to the levering action and let-off created by the cam system on a compound bow, the amount of force required to bring the bow to full draw actually increases to peak weight rather quickly before dropping off dramatically at full draw. For example, the amount of force required to draw a 45-pound compound bow set at a 29-inch draw length might increase very quickly, peaking at 45 pounds at 19 inches and then quickly dropping to just 12 pounds when fully drawn at 29 inches.

Unlike longbows and recurves, compound bows also give you the ability to modify the draw weight of the bow at each draw length simply

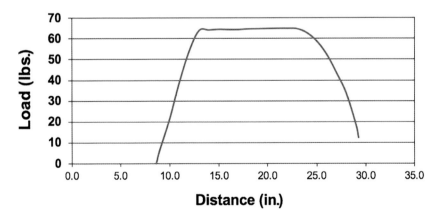

This draw-force curve illustrates the pounds of force required to draw a compound bow set at 29 inches of draw length at various points in the draw cycle. Notice how the effort required to draw the bowstring builds quickly to a maximum weight before quickly falling off as the mechanical advantage created by the levering cams takes effect. PHOTO COURTESY OF SILK OUTDOORS

On a compound bow, you can increase or decrease the draw weight of the bow at any given draw length simply by tightening or loosening the limb bolts, a procedure that increases or decreases the amount of limb flex that occurs as the bow is drawn.

by tightening or loosening the limb bolts, which changes the limb angle and either increases or decreases the amount of limb flex created during the draw cycle. Compound bows typically allow for up to 10 pounds of downward adjustment from their peak drawing weight, though some models offer a considerably larger range, as we'll discuss in a bit.

Because drawing a compound bow only requires you to exert the peak draw weight momentarily while drawing the bow and then creates let-off that allows you to hold much less weight while aiming, shooters can typically shoot a compound bow with a draw weight considerably higher than they could handle with a longbow or recurve. For example, I shoot a 45-pound recurve bow but a 60-pound compound. Again, your archery dealer will help you find a model with the right draw weight at your optimal draw length. Generally speaking, it is common for adult men to shoot 50 to 70 pounds and adult women to fall somewhere in the 30-to-50-pound range. Youth shooters often start with draw weights under 10 pounds.

BOW LENGTH

If you are looking for a longbow or recurve, you'll need to match the length of your bow to your draw length. This will result in a smooth draw and maximize the efficiency of your limbs.

MADE FOR EACH OTHER

Archery has experienced a surge in popularity in recent years, fueled largely by a tremendous influx of female and youth shooters. This is an extremely positive trend for the future of the sport, and bow manufacturers have responded with a host of new models designed with the needs of women and youths in mind. Far from "beginner" bows, many of these offerings incorporate the same designs and technologies as other top bows, only with scaled down dimensions, lighter draw weights, smaller grips, and other modifications geared toward smaller-framed shooters. Such bows also typically have eye-catching styling designed to appeal to a female archer or a youngster's high-energy attitude. If you are a woman or young person, it's definitely worth checking some of these models out; you just might discover you were made for each other!

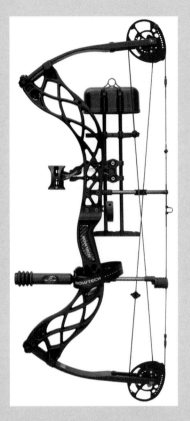

Women are among the fastest-growing segments of the archery community, and bow manufacturers are responding with tailored models such as the Carbon Rose from Bowtech Archery. PHOTO COURTESY OF BOWTECH ARCHERY

If you shoot a bow that's too short, you'll be flexing the limbs farther than they were designed to go and could possibly damage them in the process. Overdrawing the bow will also create a very severe string angle and will likely pinch your fingers, resulting in awkward releases and poor accuracy. And if you shoot a bow that's too long, you won't flex the limbs enough to store much energy.

Although many people correlate proper longbow and recurve bow length with the shooter's height, this is not always a reliable method because every person is unique and we are all proportioned a bit differently. Basing your decision on draw length is a better option, and since we've already determined your draw length, it also makes this step pretty easy.

If you are purchasing a compound bow, the length of the bow is not overly critical. However, there are still a few things to consider. The length of compound bows is measured from one cam axle to the other, which is typically referred to as "axle-to-axle length." Keep in mind that the actual length of the bow is somewhat greater, as part of the cams extend beyond the axle.

PROPER BOW LENGTH FOR LONGBOW & RECURVE SHOOTERS

Draw Length	Bow Length
14–16 in.	48 in.
18–20 in.	54 in.
20–22 in.	58 in.
22–24 in.	62 in.
24–26 in.	64 in.
26–28 in.	66 in.
28–30 in.	68 in.
30+ in.	70 in.

Compound bow lengths generally range from 28 to 40 inches, with hunting models generally falling between 28 and 34 inches and target models generally falling between 34 and 40 inches. The reason for this is that shorter axle-to-axle bows are easier to maneuver in hunting situations, while longer axle-to-axle bows tend to be easier to hold steady and are more "forgiving" of small errors in shooting form, making them well suited for competition. Longer bows also have a less severe string angle, which makes them better suited for shooting with fingers. As previously mentioned, most compound bows are drawn and released with a mechanical release aid, but those who do shoot compounds using fingers generally look for a longer axle-to-axle bow.

BOW WEIGHT

Bow weight is the physical weight of the bow itself. Longbows and traditional recurves typically weigh about 2 pounds, compounds generally weigh 4 to 5 pounds, and Olympic recurves fall in between the two. In addition to the bow itself, you'll also have to add the weight of any bow-mounted accessories, such as a sight, arrow rest, and stabilizer.

Many archers appreciate a relatively lightweight bow setup because it is easier to hold up while drawing and aiming. Heavy bows can result in increased shoulder fatigue in your bow arm after repeated shots. And bowhunters really like light bows because they are easier to carry in the woods. Bow manufacturers work hard to keep bow weight to a minimum by designing aluminum risers with numerous cutouts and rounded edges that reduce the amount of material used. In recent years they have started making some bow risers out of carbon fiber, an extremely strong but lightweight material that can reduce overall bow weight by up to 25 percent. Just keep in mind that the lightest bows are often among the most expensive due to the higher end materials used and added machine work required to produce them.

Although a lightweight bow certainly has its advantages, a heavier bow is actually more stable at full draw because the added mass makes it harder to move. That's why competitive target archers add multiple weighted stabilizers to their bows and arrange weights far out in front and behind the bow to not only add mass but also improve overall balance.

ADJUSTABILITY AND SHAREABILITY

If you are purchasing archery gear for a growing shooter, or if you have multiple family members who want to shoot but can't afford multiple bows, this section is very important. The good news is that there are many bows designed to accommodate growing shooters or even be shared among multiple users.

If you are searching for a recurve, you'll want to look for a take-down design with a riser that allows you to easily change limb sets. A young shooter just getting started will need relatively short, lightweight limbs, but new limbs can be purchased as he or she grows without replacing the entire bow or related equipment. It's also possible for multiple shooters to share a riser and shoot with different limb sets.

When it comes to compound bows, there are many models designed specifically for growing shooters—and these bows are capable of carrying them all the way from their very first shots to adulthood. For example, Diamond Archery's Infinite Edge Pro

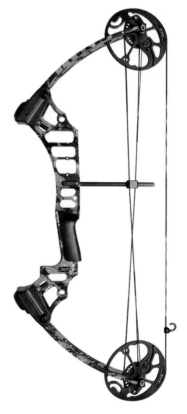

The Craze II from Mission Archery is among an increasing number of youth bow models designed to "grow" with an archer, allowing draw length and draw weight to easily be adjusted upward as the shooter grows. PHOTO COURTESY OF MISSION ARCHERY

The National Archery in Schools Program uses the Genesis bow, a special compound design with no set draw length or weight. This allows multiple students to share the same bow with no adjustments necessary. PHOTO COURTESY OF NASP

boasts an incredible draw-length range of 13 to 31 inches and a draw-weight range of 5 to 70 pounds, which means it is a bow that can easily be shot by an elementary school student or a fully grown adult. Similar models from other manufacturers, such as the Hoyt Ignite, Mission Craze II, and Bear Cruzer, mean you have plenty of options. Perhaps best of all, these bows offer impressive shooting performance at a value-oriented price and are available in a variety of trendy colors sure to please the sometimes finicky tastes of young people. I have personal experience using these types of bows with my own children and feel confident in saying they are an excellent choice for just about any young shooter.

A final type of compound bow worth mentioning here is the original Genesis from Genesis Archery. This unique compound design has no set draw length and can be shot by anyone with a draw length between 15 and 30 inches. Draw weight can be adjusted from 10 to 20 pounds, and there is no let-off, which makes it easy to shoot using fingers instead of a mechanical release aid. The Genesis truly is a compound that can be passed from one shooter to the next with no adjustments whatsoever, and that versatility is why the Genesis is the official bow of the National Archery in Schools Program, which teaches archery skills to 2 million students each year.

ROUNDING OUT YOUR SETUP

Once you've tried some bows and made your selection, you'll have to figure out what other gear you need. Of course everyone will need some arrows. But beyond that, your needs will vary depending on the type of bow you choose and how you plan to use it. For example, someone buying a traditional recurve may need a shooting tab, bow stringer, arm guard, and hip quiver, while a compound shooter will need an arrow rest, bow sight, stabilizer, mechanical release aid, and more.

I know I've mentioned archery pro shops several times already, but when it comes to purchasing your first bow, there really is no better place than a dedicated archery dealer. In addition to selling you a bow, a knowledgeable archery pro will know exactly what accessories are needed and make sure all the equipment is properly calibrated and fitted.

Most pro shops will charge a nominal "bow setup" fee when putting a new bow package together for a customer. Let me assure you that this fee, typically around $50, is one of the smartest investments you can make in your archery experience. This fee includes making any needed bow adjustments to ensure a proper fit, as well as installation and tuning of all bow accessories. During the process, your dealer will check to ensure everything is just right and even spend some time teaching you to shoot the bow properly and answering any questions you have.

Using equipment that is not properly fitted or tuned is one of the biggest reasons new archers struggle. I *guarantee* that having a professional set your bow up and show you how to use it will make your initial shooting experiences much more fun and save you a lot of headaches down the road—which is exactly where we're headed. The next chapter offers a brief but important look at basic archery safety rules. Then we'll be ready to start shooting!

CHAPTER 4
Safety First

"NOW WAIT A MINUTE."

Oh, how I hated to hear those words uttered by my fishing buddy, Mike. I spent many days on the water with Mike and always looked forward to our adventures with great anticipation. Finally, the weekend would arrive and I'd head over to Mike's house itching to get on the

A NOTE TO PARENTS

Ensuring your children enjoy a safe archery shooting experience is ultimately your responsibility, and it's up to you to make sure your children understand the basics of safe shooting *and* practice them. Younger children should be supervised at all times when shooting, and older children should be supervised until they have demonstrated a solid understanding of safe shooting rules and a commitment to following them. I am not going to provide any hard-and-fast age guidelines for shooting supervision, since each child is different. Ultimately, it is up to you as a parent to decide what is appropriate.

Parents have a responsibility to teach safe shooting practices to their children—and hold them accountable for abiding by them.

I also encourage you to adopt a "zero tolerance" policy when it comes to dangerous behavior and horseplay on the archery range. Having fun is the goal, but *never* at the expense of safety. Remind your children that having access to a bow and arrows is a privilege, not a right, and those who violate safe shooting rules must lose that privilege out of respect for fellow shooters.

water. Just as the boat trailer was hooked up and I thought we were finally ready to head out, Mike would utter those four words I came to dread. I was just ready to **GO**, while Mike wanted to head back into the garage one last time to make sure he hadn't forgotten anything important that we'd need during our outing.

Right now, I imagine you are in much the same place. You've just learned the basics of archery equipment and how to get yourself properly outfitted with a bow of your own. You're excited about that new bow, and, by golly, you want to go shoot!

ARCHERY RANGE WHISTLE COMMANDS

Archery events from professional tournaments to beginning archery classes employ a standardized set of whistle commands to control the range and ensure safe shooting:

2 Whistle Blasts: Archers may proceed from the waiting line to the shooting line.

1 Whistle Blast: Archers may place an arrow on the string and start shooting.

3 Whistle Blasts: The "all-clear" signal that archers may walk downrange and pull their arrows from the target.

5 or More Whistle Blasts: Emergency. Stop shooting immediately; remove all arrows from your bow and place them in your quiver.

On formal archery ranges, shooting is often controlled by a range master who manages the action by way of standard whistle commands.

Trust me, I know *exactly* how you feel. And I know the last thing you want to do now—right as we're getting to the really good part—is stop and read a long, boring chapter on safety. Still, as with all shooting sports, safety must be paramount when shooting a bow and arrow, and I'd be doing you a disservice if I didn't address it now. However, I promise I'll make this a relatively short and not-so-boring chapter that tells you what you need to know and gets you flinging arrows in almost no time.

SAFETY IS NO ACCIDENT

The good news is that archery is one of the safest sports you can participate in. In fact, analysis of injury data from the US Consumer Product Safety Commission and the Sporting Goods Manufacturers Association indicates that archery has an injury rate of fewer than 1 per 1,000 participants. In comparison, activities such as golf and fishing have injury rates about twice as high as archery, while popular ball sports such as soccer, baseball, and football have injury rates 15 to 25 times higher than archery. Archery's safety statistics are even more impressive when you consider the fact that so many of America's estimated 17 million archers are children with little or no prior shooting experience. The National Archery in Schools Program, for example, has taught archery to millions of students since its inception in 2002 without ever reporting a single accident.

Still, there is some inherent danger in archery, since an errant arrow from even a lightweight traditional bow can cause serious injury. Shooting in archery classes and organized competitions typically takes place under the supervision of a range master who ensures safe practices and controls shooting using a series of standard whistle commands. However, for the purposes of this book, I assume you'll do a lot of your shooting with family and friends in your backyard or some other informal setting where you need to take responsibility for your own safety and the safety of others in the area. Knowing the commonsense safety practices outlined here, and practicing them *every time* you shoot, will help you avoid injury and/or damage to your archery equipment and property.

RULE 1: CHECK YOUR EQUIPMENT

The first rule of archery safety is to check your bow and arrows for damage before every shooting session. A quick visual inspection of your bow will reveal any major defects, such as a cracked limb or partially frayed string or cable. If any obvious problems are discovered, *do not* shoot the bow, which can result in permanent damage to the bow and possibly

Visually inspect your bow and arrows before every shooting session. A frayed bowstring such as this is a serious issue and not safe to shoot. Instead, visit your local archery dealer for needed repairs before shooting.

You can inspect carbon arrows for cracks by lightly flexing them in your hands, a procedure that will typically reveal any small fractures in the carbon fiber.

flying debris that can cause serious injury. Instead, take it to your local archery dealer for repair.

Arrows should be similarly inspected. Aluminum arrows that are bent should be discarded. Carbon arrows should be carefully inspected for cracks, especially after any errant shots that result in hard impacts. Any large cracks in carbon arrows are usually obvious, and hairline fractures can typically be identified by lightly flexing the shaft in your hands. Quite common, but not always readily seen, are small cracks at the front and rear ends of the shaft. Look carefully at the shaft ends near your practice points and nocks, and if any small cracks are discovered, discard those arrows immediately. Shooting fractured carbon arrows can result in the arrow splintering upon release of the string, causing serious injury to the shooter and others nearby.

RULE 2: NEVER NOCK AN ARROW UNTIL THE RANGE IS CLEAR

Whenever you shoot, always make sure the range (the area between you and your target) is clear of other people, pets, etc., before you place an arrow on your bowstring, and pay attention to make sure the range remains clear throughout your shooting session.

If you are shooting with other archers, use a designated shooting line and ensure that no one moves forward of other shooters into the line of fire. Any spectators should stand well behind shooters, and if a person or animal enters the range, shooting must stop immediately and all shooters should remove their arrows from their bows. If someone is at full draw when a person or animal enters the range, that shooter should immediately point his or her bow toward the ground and carefully let down the bowstring.

Never shoot until the range—the area between you and your target—is clear.

RULE 3: ALWAYS POINT YOUR BOW IN A SAFE DIRECTION

You must keep your bow pointed in a safe direction—downrange toward the target—whenever an arrow is nocked on your bowstring. ***Never*** point your bow at another person, animal, building, or vehicle.

RULE 4: ONLY SHOOT ARCHERY TARGETS

Never shoot your bow at anything other than designated archery targets capable of safely stopping your arrows without damaging them. You also must ensure there is a sufficient backstop and/or buffer zone beyond your target to ensure that any errant arrows cannot leave the range area and cause injury or damage to people, pets, buildings, or other property. It's also worth noting that wildlife such as songbirds, squirrels, rabbits, and chipmunks are ***NOT*** targets.

RULE 5: NEVER SHOOT AN ARROW DIRECTLY UP IN THE AIR

This commonsense rule goes with No. 4 above. Never give into the temptation to release a random arrow into the air just to "see how far it can go" or for any other reason. This is extremely dangerous—arrows shot in this manner can travel great distances and accidentally strike unintended targets.

RULE 6: DO NOT RUN WITH YOUR ARCHERY GEAR

Never run while holding your bow and/or arrows, as any falls can result in injury to yourself and damage to your gear. Instead, walk as you move from one shooting location to another and when moving to and from your shooting location to your target to retrieve arrows.

RULE 7: RETRIEVE ARROWS PROPERLY

Shooters should never proceed downrange to retrieve arrows until all shooting has stopped and everyone agrees that the range is clear. To properly remove an arrow from a target, place your hand around the shaft directly against the target and pull straight backward from the arrow's angle of entry. Sometimes arrows can be difficult to remove, so a variety of arrow pullers are available to increase your leverage. However, the same method should be used even with an arrow puller. Never attempt to remove an arrow from the target by grabbing the shaft back away from

Always point your bow downrange toward the target.

Only shoot into archery targets specifically designed to safely and effectively stop your arrows.

the target; this results in a great amount of arrow flex during removal, which can bend and/or break the shaft. When removing arrows from a target, it is also important to take turns and allow just one person at a time to retrieve his or her arrows. Other shooters should stand several feet back to avoid being poked with an arrow as the person retrieving arrows pulls them out of the target.

Finally, in the case of errant arrows that travel beyond the target, all shooters should help search for those arrows and ensure that everyone is safely clear of the range before shooting resumes.

The proper way to remove your arrows from a target is to grab the shaft directly up against the target and pull directly rearward from the arrow's angle of entry.

HOUSE RULES

In addition to the universal guidelines addressed here, you are likely to have some "house rules" when it comes to safety where you shoot. Such rules could include avoiding neighbors' property lines, restricting shooting to certain hours to avoid conflict with other activities in the area, or equipment limitations (such as a 20-pound maximum draw weight) due to the type of target you are using or a somewhat smaller buffer zone beyond the target. Again, you must use common sense to anticipate potential dangers and adopt rules to eliminate it. As the old saying goes, an ounce of prevention is worth a pound of cure.

Now, let's start shooting!

CHAPTER 5
Your First Shots

New shooters should start out close to the target and gradually move back as skills improve. Short shots up the odds of hitting the mark, and that generates even more excitement and enthusiasm.

AS YOU PREPARE TO TAKE YOUR FIRST SHOTS, I'd like to let you in on a little secret: Shooting a bow is simple. You place an arrow on the string, draw, aim, and release. The arrow sails magically into flight and, voilà, you're an archer! That's really all there is to it.

Oh, I know what you're thinking; *surely* it's more complicated than that. After all, if it's so easy, how come we need an entire book to learn the sport? Well, there *are* certain fundamentals to good shooting. And

BE ON GUARD!

Before you grab your bow and hit the range, remember to put on your arm guard! The guard will protect your bow arm if the bowstring hits it after the arrow is released. This impact, commonly referred to as "string slap" or "bow bite," can be quite painful and cause redness and even bruising if an arm guard is not used. Although not all archers will have a problem with string slap—and the string stoppers on many newer compound bows have significantly reduced the problem—I highly recommend that all new archers start shooting with an arm guard and continue using it until they are confident that string slap will not be an issue.

Wearing an arm guard while shooting will protect your forearm from abrasions or bruising that can occur if the bowstring slaps your forearm during the shot.

becoming a world-class archer requires many years of dedication, learning, and refinement—not to mention a whole lot of natural skill! But that doesn't change my point that archery is beautiful in its simplicity. And as a new archer, I want you to embrace that concept. Whether you are 5, 95, or somewhere in between, you can do this and learn to do it well.

This chapter will walk you through seven steps of a basic shot sequence that will form the foundation of your shooting routine. As with any athletic endeavor, the key to successful bow shooting is learning the proper method and then repeating it over and over and over again until it becomes automatic. Although I have done my best to make the instructions as clear as possible, I encourage you to refer to the accompanying photos to ensure that you are using proper form.

In future chapters we'll take a closer look at these steps and provide additional insights to help refine your shooting technique and improve your accuracy. But right now, we are just focusing on the basics, and I encourage you to relax, have fun, and not worry about where your arrows hit the target—or even whether they hit the target at all, for that matter. I also encourage you to take your first shots from a very close range. Those shooting with young children may want to start with the target as little as 5 feet away, and even for a group of new adult shooters, an initial shot distance no greater than 10 yards is recommended. You should feel free to increase shot distance as you progress, but at this early stage, it is much more important to focus on the process than the result. After all, not even Robin Hood could hit the bull's-eye his first day of practice!

> STEP 1
FIND YOUR STANCE

Stance refers to how you stand in relation to the target when shooting the bow. A good stance provides a solid foundation for your body and helps minimize movement while aiming. Less movement means more accuracy.

The best starting stance for new shooters is called the "neutral stance." To assume a neutral stance, begin by straddling a line parallel to your target. If you are shooting on an indoor archery range, there is likely an established "shooting line" painted on the floor. If you are shooting outside, you can use a piece of string or simply scratch a line in the dirt as a point of reference. Place one foot on either side of the line, about shoulder width apart, with your weight evenly distributed on each foot and the shoulder of your bow arm pointing directly toward the target. For a right-handed shooter, this means the left shoulder is pointed downrange

The best stance for new shooters is the "neutral stance" shown here, with your feet shoulder width apart, your weight distributed evenly on each foot, and the shoulder of your bow arm pointed toward the target.

These photos show an archer in a proper neutral stance (left) compared to an improper head-on stance (right).

toward the target. For a left-handed shooter, this means the right shoulder will be pointed downrange. For most people, the toe of the back foot will be slightly in front of the toe of the front foot when standing in the neutral stance. You also want to keep your knees slightly bent, not locked fully upright.

When standing in the neutral position with your head facing straight ahead, you will be looking perpendicular to the target. If you are inside, you will be staring straight at the side wall of the range. Because of this, many new shooters want to stand facing directly toward the target to shoot. However, this is an improper stance that results in poor bow alignment on target and poor accuracy. Refer to the accompanying photo illustrations to ensure you have found your neutral stance.

> STEP 2
NOCK THE ARROW

"Nock" is one of those funny archery words that is both a noun and a verb. The nock is the little plastic piece at the back end of your arrow that attaches to the bowstring, and placing the arrow on the string is commonly referred to as "nocking" an arrow.

As we discussed in the previous chapter, never nock an arrow on your string until the range is clear and you are ready to shoot. To properly

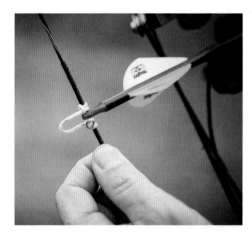

To properly nock an arrow, simply slide the groove of the nock onto the bowstring until it clicks into place.

load the arrow, place the nock below the nocking point on your string or in the center of your nocking loop and gently press it onto the string until it clicks into place.

Nocks should fit on the bowstring snugly but not too tight. Nocks that fit too loosely can result in arrows coming off the string while drawing or at full draw, which could result in a potentially dangerous dry fire. Nocks that fit too tightly will cause excessive string wear and also result in inconsistent arrow launch and diminished accuracy. A good way to test for proper nock fit on your bowstring is to nock an arrow and then hold the bow parallel to the ground with the arrow pointing downward. The arrow should be held securely on the string as it dangles off the bow but fall off easily if you tap the bowstring. If the arrow falls off on its own when the bow is pointed toward the ground, the nock fit is too loose. If the arrow will not fall off the string with a firm tap on the string, the nock fit is too tight. Your local archery dealer can help solve problems with improper nock fit by either replacing the nocks on your arrows or replacing the center serving on your bowstring with wider or narrower thread as needed to ensure proper nock tension. Your center serving is the section of thread wound tightly around your bowstring in its center where the arrow attaches. This thread protects the bowstring itself from excess wear and also allows for nock fit to be adjusted by employing narrower or wider thread, as needed.

A final consideration when nocking your arrows is to ensure that the vanes or feathers are properly oriented for your bow. For example, on

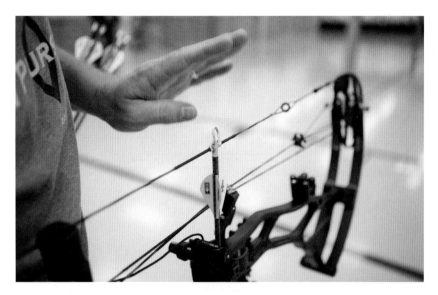

You can check for proper nock fit simply by pointing your arrow toward the ground and tapping the bowstring. If the arrow falls off the string with only a light tap, the nock fit is too loose; if the arrow will not come off the bowstring with a firm tap on the bowstring, the nock fit is likely too tight.

most traditional bows you will want to nock arrows with the odd-colored feather ("cock" feather) pointing out away from the bow and the two same-colored feathers ("hen" feathers) facing in toward the riser to minimize contact with the riser. On most Olympic recurve and compound bows, you will want to nock arrows with the odd-colored feather or vane pointed up to avoid contact with the arrow rest. Unless the nocks on your arrows are glued in place, you should be able to gently rotate them inside the shaft to ensure proper vane orientation for your bow. A small plastic nock wrench is helpful for adjusting vane orientation.

A small plastic nock wrench is a handy tool for adjusting the rotation of your nock inside the shaft to achieve proper vane orientation.

SET YOUR GRIP AND RELEASE HAND

Once an arrow is nocked on your bowstring, you are ready to set your grip and release hand. Interestingly, although the area where you hold the bow while shooting is called the "grip," you really don't want to

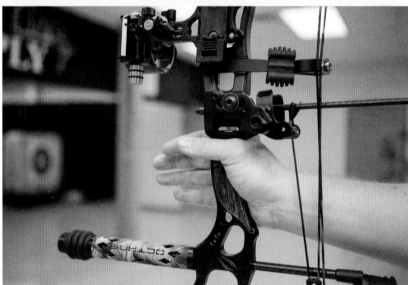

Rather than tightly squeezing the bow's grip, you want to gently cradle the handle and allow the tension of the bowstring to push the bow into the V-shaped notch between your thumb and forefinger, as shown here.

grip it. Gripping the bow tightly while shooting causes sideways torque as you aim and release the arrow, resulting in erratic arrow flight. Rather than holding tightly to the bow's grip, you want to cradle it gently as you draw, aim, and release, allowing the tension created by the drawn bowstring to press the bow into the base of your palm below the V-shaped notched between your thumb and index finger.

Along with ensuring proper hand placement on the bow, you'll also set your release hand at this point. For those shooting with fingers, a good starting point is to use three fingers below the arrow for traditional bows and one finger above the arrow and two below for Olympic recurves. If you are a compound shooter using a mechanical release aid, now is when you'll attach the jaw or hook of your release to the bowstring or nocking loop.

These photos, top to bottom, demonstrate the proper method for setting the release hand for archers shooting traditional bows, Olympic-style recurve bows, and compound bows.

RAISE, DRAW, AND ANCHOR

Now, with you bow hand properly set on the grip and your release hand either holding the bowstring or hooked on via your release aid, raise the bow to eye level, keeping the arrow pointed downrange toward your target.

Once your release hand is set, slowly raise your bow to eye level as demonstrated here.

This overhead photo illustrates proper "T" form at full draw, with the bow arm pointed directly toward the target and the release arm pointed directly away from it.

Next, slowly bring the bowstring back until the hand of your drawing arm reaches your face. Focus on keeping the arrow pointed toward the target as you draw the bowstring in one smooth, fluid motion, keeping the elbow of your drawing arm level with the ground and pointed directly away from your bow arm so that your body forms a "T." You also want to hold your head naturally upright and turned toward the target during the draw. If your bow is properly fitted, you should not have to crane your neck forward or tilt it backward to align with the bowstring. The elbow of your bow arm should be straight but not hyperextended.

For those shooting traditional bows, the most common anchor position is to place the knuckle at the base of your index finger against your cheekbone.

For archers who shoot Olympic-style recurve bows, the most common anchor point is the jawline.

Finally, with the bowstring pulled all the way back, find your anchor point. For those shooting traditional bows, the most common anchor position is to place the knuckle at the base of your index finger against your cheekbone.

For those shooting Olympic recurves, the anchor point is generally at the jawline; some shooting tabs designed for use with Olympic recurves have small extensions designed to be pressed into the jawbone at full draw.

For compound bow shooters using a release aid, one of the most common anchor points is to place the knuckle at the base of the index finger into the small depression at the base of the ear, just behind the earlobe. In addition to anchoring the release hand on the face, compound shooters will also need to make sure they anchor in a position that allows them to see through the peep sight. Many compound shooters find they are able

For compound bow shooters using a release aid, the most common anchor point is to place the knuckle at the base of the index finger into the small depression at the base of the ear, just behind the earlobe.

to gently touch the tip of their nose to the bowstring while looking through the peep sight at full draw. This provides a secondary reference point, as does a kisser button (if used), which should align with the crease between your lips at the corner of the mouth.

Regardless of the style of bow you shoot or the anchor point you choose, it *must* remain consistent shot after shot in order to achieve consistent accuracy.

> STEP 5

AIM

With your drawing hand anchored, it is now time to aim. The aiming process will vary depending on the type of bow you shoot. If you are shooting a traditional longbow or recurve, aiming is an instinctive process that will take time to develop as you gain familiarity with your bow's performance. As a starting point, simply look down the shaft of your arrow and point the arrow at the spot on the target you want to hit. Based on the result of that initial shot, you will then mentally calculate how much higher or lower you need to aim on subsequent shots to hit your mark. Of course those adjustments will change as shot distance changes. It truly is a trial-and-error process, and your ability to hit the target will improve as your mind not only becomes more accustomed to the aiming process but also learns the trajectory of your arrows and becomes better able to estimate how high or low to hold the bow at various distances.

When shooting a traditional longbow or recurve, aim by looking down the arrow shaft and lining it up with the target.

Those shooting Olympic recurves will aim using the small aperture on the bow sight, placing the pin inside the aperture where you want the arrow to hit. The aperture serves as the front aiming reference, while the bowstring serves as a rear aiming reference to ensure proper bow alignment. Most Olympic recurve shooters align the bowstring just inside the sight aperture. As you aim, keep the position of the string steady in relation to the aperture. You should be able to see it in the periphery of your vision as you stare at the target.

Most Olympic recurve shooters align the bowstring just inside the sight aperture while aiming. You should be able to see it in the periphery of your vision as you stare at the target.

Those shooting compound bows will look through the peep sight in their string and then place the sight pin where they want the arrow to hit. For compound shooters, the peep sight serves as the rear aiming reference and the sight serves as the front

Those shooting compound bows will look through the peep sight in their string and then place the sight pin where they want the arrow to hit.

aiming reference to ensure proper bow alignment. When looking through the peep sight, center the circular pin housing of your sight inside the circular opening of the peep and then place the pin on target. By keeping the pin housing centered in the peep opening, you will maintain proper bow alignment on target and use the same anchor point on each shot regardless of distance or which pin inside the housing you are aiming with.

LET IT FLOAT!

If you are shooting a bow with a sight, one thing you will notice as you aim is that it is impossible to hold the pin completely still on the target. This is perfectly natural! In fact, not even world-champion archers can hold completely still. The key to making good shots is **NOT** trying to hold the pin perfectly steady on target or releasing the arrow at the very instant the pin passes the bull's-eye. Rather, the key is to simply **KEEP AIMING** continually as you allow the

As you aim, you will notice that the pin never holds completely still. Simply allow the aiming dot to "float" around the spot you want to hit as you execute the shot. PHOTO COURTESY OF PETERSEN'S BOWHUNTING

pin to gently float. As the pin moves away from the center of the target, simply focus on bringing it back over and over again as you aim, release, and follow-through. This focus on aiming *instead* of shooting will help reinforce good form and lead to consistent accuracy.

HOW TO ADJUST YOUR BOW SIGHT

If you had your bow set up by your local archery shop, your sight should be at least close to on target. However, it is likely you will have to make some minor tweaks once you settle into a consistent shooting form. And if you are installing a new sight yourself, you need to know how to properly set it up so that your aim is true.

Although the sights generally used on compound and Olympic recurve bows vary in design and appearance, the principles for properly calibrating them are the same. Simply put, every sight offers adjustment options that will allow you to move your pin or pins up, down, left, and right. Depending on the particular sight on your bow, this may be accomplished by loosening setscrews and sliding parts of the sight around or by loosening setscrews and turning small dials that allow for more precise microadjustments. Regardless, the same task is accomplished.

When moving your pin, here's the only rule you need to know: **FOLLOW YOUR ARROW.** This means that if your arrow hits low, you will move your pin down. If your arrow hits high, you will move your pin up. If your arrow hits left, you will move your pin left. If your arrow hits right, you will move your pin right.

Before you make *any* adjustments to your sight, you need to confirm that you are shooting consistently by grouping arrows in the same area. If you can group three to five arrows together, you can then adjust your sight to bring the arrows in toward the center of the bull's-eye. But if you cannot shoot a decent group, it is impossible to know where to move your pins. The inability to group arrows even at close range is the result of poor shooting form, poorly tuned equipment—or both. If you cannot figure out the problem and shoot decent arrow groups, I recommend a visit to the local archery shop for professional assistance.

Assuming you have decent arrow groups but simply aren't on target, what follows is a step-by-step method for bringing your arrows into the bull's-eye. If you are starting from scratch, I recommend making your initial adjustments from a distance of 10 yards. If your sight is already partially calibrated and your

If you are shooting good arrow groups but the arrows are not hitting where your sight is aimed, you can adjust your sight pins to compensate.

arrows are hitting reasonably close to center, it's OK to start at 20 yards.

1. Start by placing a strip of masking tape vertically across the center of your target. Your goal will be to hit this tape while shooting.
2. Shoot three arrows at the tape and see where they land. Do not worry about how high or low your arrows hit; just focus on whether they hit to the left or right of the tape.
3. If your arrows are hitting to the left of the tape, you need to move your pin to the left. If they are hitting to the right, you need to move your pin to the right. Use the adjustment on your sight to move the pin or pins in the desired direction, and then retighten the setscrew to prevent further movement.
4. Shoot three more arrows at the vertical tape. You should either be hitting the tape now or at least be closer than you were before. Continue making incremental left/right pin adjustments until you are hitting the tape. If you go too far and your arrows begin hitting on the other side of the tape, simply make a small adjustment back toward where your pin started. Just remember to always follow your arrows with your pin. Once your arrows are centered on the tape, the left/right setting of your sight is properly calibrated and you can move on to Step 5.
5. Remove the vertical tape from your target and place a piece of masking tape horizontally across the center of your target.

If your arrows are hitting to the left or right of where you are aiming, you can move your pins left or right to bring the impact point into proper alignment.

6. Shoot three arrows at the tape and see where they land. During this phase, do not worry about the side-to-side placement of your arrows; just focus on whether they hit above or below the tape.

7. If your arrows are hitting above the tape, you will need to move your pin up. If your arrows are hitting below the tape, you will need to move your pin down. If you are using a multi-pin sight, use the "gang" adjustment screw to move your entire pin guard up and down until the height of your top pin is correct. You can later set your lower pins using the individual pin adjustment screws.

8. Shoot three more arrows at the horizontal tape. You should either be hitting the tape or be closer than you were before. Continue making incremental vertical adjustments to your pin until your arrows hit the tape, always keeping in mind to follow the impact point of your arrows with your pin. Once your arrows are hitting the vertical tape, the elevation setting of your pin (or top pin on multi-pin sights) is properly calibrated for **THAT DISTANCE** only. For example, if you sighted in at 20 yards, that pin is now sighted in for 20 yards.

9. If you are shooting a single-pin sight, you still need to figure out how much to lower your pin for longer-range shots. Most single-pin sights have hashmarks or white tapes where you can indicate where to "dial" the pin depending on the yardage. If you are shooting a multi-pin sight, you need to move back to the desired ranges for your other pins (30 yards, 40 yards, etc.) and set them via trial and error until the gaps between your pins are properly spaced for your desired distances.

If your arrows are hitting higher or lower than where you are aiming, you can move your sight pin up or down to bring the impact point into proper alignment.

When using a multi-pin sight, you need to adjust the elevation of each pin for a desired range—20 yards, 30 yards, 40 yards, etc.

That's pretty much it! Calibrating a sight is not complicated, and you will become more comfortable with the process as you work through it. However, there are two quick notes I want to add before we move on.

First, one common issue new archers have after calibrating their sight pins is shooting again a day or two later, only to find their arrows are no longer hitting the bull's-eye. The reason for this is that many archers make small variations in their form from day to day without even realizing it. Today's archery equipment is even more reliable and consistent than we are, and while it's tempting to immediately begin playing with your sight after a few errant shots, in almost all cases it is **YOU** who has changed, not your bow. For this reason, I recommend putting in at least several shooting sessions and verifying any discrepancies before making additional pin adjustments. Many times I have had an "off" day where my arrows were not on target only to shoot again the next day and be right back in the bull's-eye.

Second, you should find that your arrows are centered left/right on the target regardless of shot range. If you find that your arrows are dead center at 10 or 20 yards but drifting well to the left or right of the bull's-eye at longer ranges, this is likely a problem with the left/right setting on your arrow rest. This problem can typically be corrected via a method called "walk-back tuning," which your local archery shop can do. There are a number of online articles and videos demonstrating the walk-back tuning method if you experience this issue and want to take a shot at resolving it yourself.

> STEP 6
RELEASE

Just as the name implies, the release is when you let the bowstring go and the arrow is launched. It is important to continue aiming and keep your focus on the target as you release and the arrow leaves the bow.

When shooting with fingers, you don't want to consciously trigger the shot. Rather, simply let your fingers relax until the string leaves on its own.

For those shooting traditional and Olympic recurve bows with fingers, releasing the arrow involves nothing more than allowing your fingers to relax on the bowstring, which results in the taut bowstring slipping from your fingers and springing forward. You don't want to consciously trigger the shot with a flick of your fingers but rather simply let your fingers relax until the string leaves on its own. An accomplished recurve shooter described a good finger release to me this way: "It's the difference between letting go and not holding on anymore."

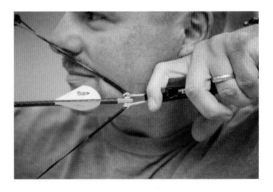

Compound bow shooters should not yank on the trigger of their release aid. Instead, focus on the target as you pull your rear elbow farther and farther back with your finger curled around the trigger.

For compound shooters using a trigger-activated release aid, continue aiming and holding the sight pin on target as you slowly increase trigger tension until the shot fires. As with finger shooters, the key to a good release lies not in consciously commanding the moment of the shot but rather in continuing to aim as you gradually pull through the shot until the release opens. Instead of yanking on the trigger, focus on the target as you pull your rear elbow farther and farther back with your finger curled around the trigger. Think about bringing your shoulder blades together in your back. This will steadily increase pressure on the trigger and—if done properly—result in a shot that almost takes you by surprise.

FOLLOW THROUGH

Once the string is released and the arrow leaps from the bow, you may think your job is done. However, good follow-through is critical to accurate shooting. Although it seems as though the arrow is gone from the bow almost instantaneously, there is in fact just enough time for you to negatively impact arrow flight.

We will discuss much more about the importance of follow-through and the problems poor follow-through causes in chapter 10. For now, however, I will simply tell you to focus on maintaining your shooting form and holding your bow hand, bow arm, and head still from the time the string is released until you see and/or hear the arrow hit the target. Resist the temptation to crane your neck sideways at the shot in an effort to get a better view of your arrow in flight (a common shooting flaw known as "peeking").

"Peeking" is a common flaw in shooting form that results when an archer moves the bow arm out of the way at the instant the bowstring is released in an effort to get a better look at the arrow in flight. The result is erratic arrow flight and poor accuracy.

FIND YOUR RHYTHM

I've tried to keep my description of each step in the shot cycle as short and simple as possible, but it is still a lot to digest for new shooters. That's why at the beginning of the chapter, I encouraged you to focus more on the process than the result. If you are a beginning archer, chances are you are using muscles not accustomed to heavy use and standing in positions that might feel a bit awkward at first. My best advice at this stage is to take things slowly and proceed at your own pace.

Because this book is geared toward families, it is also important to recognize that groups of new shooters of various ages and abilities will advance at different rates. It is entirely possible that a teenage or adult shooter will improve quite rapidly while younger children will likely need more time to learn the basics. Allow each member of the family to progress at his or her own pace.

I also think it's worth offering a word of encouragement here to parents who may find teaching their younger children all the fundamentals in this chapter a daunting task. My advice on this count is: *Don't sweat the small stuff.* As long as your children are shooting *safely* and *having fun*, I wouldn't worry too much about the finer points of their shooting form.

Illustration by Caroline Design

HOW LONG SHOULD A SHOT TAKE?

New archers often wonder how long it should take them to make a shot. While there is no exact answer to that question, a good rule is that you want to complete the entire shot sequence within about 8 seconds.

Why 8 seconds? Basically it boils down to muscle fatigue and your ability to maintain proper form. If you cannot draw your bow, anchor, aim, release, and follow through within roughly 8 seconds, your muscles will tire and your form will begin to break down, manifesting itself in poor accuracy.

If you don't feel comfortable at full draw, there is nothing wrong with slowly letting the string down, taking a few deep breaths, and starting over. Professional shooters do this all the time because they have learned that the easiest way to eliminate poor shots is to never take them in the first place.

Archery is a sport that can be enjoyed simultaneously by people of all ages and ability levels. The key is to have fun while allowing each person to progress at his or her own pace.

You may also find it easier to keep things as simple as possible at first and then slowly introduce additional concepts or equipment. For example, I introduced both my boys to archery at younger than 5 years old with a simple fiberglass recurve bow. Later, after introducing them to the compound bow, I encouraged them to continue shooting instinctively with fingers. It was only after they demonstrated an established comfort level and confidence with this method that I introduced a peep sight, bow sight, and mechanical release aid into the equation.

As we move along, we'll take a closer look at the ins and outs of shooting and provide greater detail and additional insights designed to help you improve and advance in your shooting. The photos in each chapter will help make the material as clear as possible, but as I have mentioned several times, you should not hesitate to seek personal advice from your local archery dealer. Many pro shops have certified archery coaches on staff and offer a variety of clinics, classes, and individual lessons to help resolve any issues you may encounter.

CHAPTER 6

Fine-tuning Your Stance

As you can see here, different archers will employ slightly different stances, based on their bodies' natural movement and the type of equipment used.

As mentioned in the previous chapter, a proper stance provides a stable foundation that minimizes movement while drawing, aiming, and shooting. A good stance helps minimize side-to-side and back-and-forth sway. The less your body moves during the shot, the more accurately and consistently you'll shoot.

Much of what I want to share about optimizing your stance comes courtesy of professional target archer Randy Ulmer. Randy is one of the most accomplished compound bow target shooters in history, with

Preloading occurs when you build tension in your torso while drawing and aiming your bow. This tension results in bow torque upon release and inconsistent accuracy. To understand this concept, draw your bow and swivel to the left or right of the target, feeling the tension build in your torso as you do so. CHRISTIAN BERG PHOTO

seven world titles and countless national and tournament championships under his belt. Randy is also one of the most successful bowhunters in North America and writes a regular column on better shooting for *Petersen's Bowhunting* magazine. As the magazine's editor, I've been fortunate to develop a friendship with Randy and continually benefit from his archery insights.

As Randy explains, many archers are unaware of just how much they move while shooting. To observe this, stand behind an archer and line his or her head up with a distant landmark while the archer is at full draw. Then, while holding perfectly still yourself, note how much the archer's head moves in relation to that landmark as he or she aims and releases the arrow. You can have a friend or family member do the same for you and provide feedback on how much you move while shooting.

According to Randy, the reason archers tend to move so much is that we rely too much on our muscles, which require active use to hold steady and are prone to fatigue quickly. To achieve the ideal form, we should instead rely on a posture that places most of the stress on our skeletal structure, which works passively.

When it comes to stance, standing perpendicular to the target with your feet about shoulder width apart, your knees slightly bent, and your hips tilted slightly forward provides a very stable platform that relies on the bones of the feet, legs, and hips to remain steady much more than it relies upon muscles.

A good stance also helps us keep our bow pointed at the target with no "preloading," or torque. To understand the concept of preloading, draw your bow and then move your bow arm far left of the target and aim there. You will feel tension build in your core as you swing left; after you release the arrow, your upper body will act like a preloaded spring that naturally wants to return to its resting position pointed directly at the target. You will experience the same thing if you draw and then aim far right of the target.

FINDING YOUR NEUTRAL STANCE

Randy and most other top archery instructors believe the ideal foot position is a neutral stance that produces no right or left preloading of the torso at full draw. The neutral stance described in the previous chapter is a good starting point, but you may find that your neutral stance is a bit different than fellow archers' due to your body type and/or the type of equipment you are using.

To determine your personal neutral stance, assume your normal stance, close your eyes, and then draw your bow and anchor. With your eyes still closed, swing the bow a little to the left and then a little to the right then settle into the most comfortable, relaxed position you can find. When you open your eyes, your bow/arrow should be pointed directly at the target. If it isn't, adjust your foot position slightly and repeat this process until you find the foot position that results in perfect target alignment with no preloading. Once you do, remember your foot position relative to the target—this is your neutral stance.

OPEN AND SQUARE STANCES

The neutral stance works best for most compound bow shooters. However, some archers—particularly those shooting recurves and longbows—prefer a more "open" stance. An open stance is so named because it opens up the shooter's torso to slightly face the target. Starting from the neutral stance, a right-handed shooter can open up his or her stance by moving the left (front) foot farther left of a line to the target. A left-handed shooter can open up his or her stance by moving the right (front) foot farther right of a line to the target. In either case, the result will be the torso pivoting slightly to face the target. You can vary the amount you open your stance simply by experimenting with the position of your front foot. One of the biggest advantages of an open stance for those shooting recurves and longbows is that it provides additional string clearance away from the body. Some archers also

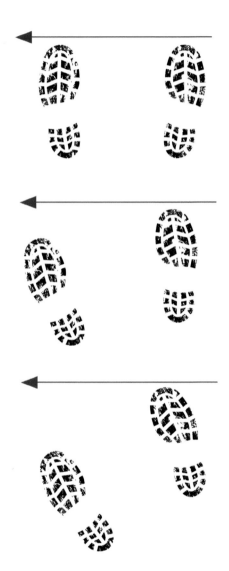

From top, this graphic shows foot positioning for the square, neutral, and open stances for a right-handed archer. The red arrow points toward the target.

PHOTO COURTESY OF PETERSEN'S BOWHUNTING

feel an open stance provides a more stable shooting position, particularly in windy conditions.

On the other end of the spectrum is a "square" stance. Rather than opening up, the square stance is closed. To find your square stance, simply place the toes of both your feet on a line that extends directly to the center of the target.

The neutral stance you found in the previous section of this chapter should be somewhere in between the open and square stances described here.

FINDING YOUR IDEAL STANCE

What is your ideal stance? There is an exercise you can use to find out. Start with a clean, three-spot bull's-eye target at 20 yards, and shoot one arrow at each spot. Shoot the first arrow using an open stance, the second arrow using a neutral stance, and the third arrow using a square stance.

Repeat this process fifteen times. You can vary which bull's-eye you aim at first, but always use the same stance for each spot. Finally, examine your group for each stance. The one with the best group is your best stance.

From there, you can simply tweak things by making slight adjustments in your foot position, getting a little more open or a little more closed, until you find your most accurate and forgiving stance.

You can determine your ideal stance simply by experimenting with different stances and determining which one produces the best accuracy.

CHAPTER 7
More on Drawing and Anchoring

AS ALREADY NOTED, THE KEY TO BECOMING A GOOD ARCHER is not simply learning to do things the right way but also being able to repeat them over and over and over again. Because of this, rhythm is critical to success. The best archers in the world have a noticeable rhythm as they execute each step of the shot process, while struggling archers have a noticeable lack of rhythm as they continually search for the "right feel" and vary their form from shot to shot.

The steps you take as you set your grip, raise the bow, draw, and anchor play a critical role in developing your shot rhythm, so I urge you to spend some time working on these things. A good drawing and anchoring sequence keeps you on target and sets you up for a successful shot.

THE PRE-DRAW

In the last chapter on stance, we discussed how using our bones instead of our muscles creates a more stable shooting platform. You can benefit from the same principle when it comes to your bow hand. We already talked about not "gripping the grip," but this is so important it is worth mentioning again. Slow-motion video has proven over and over just how important a relaxed bow hand is to accuracy. When setting your bow hand on the grip, you want to position it so that the grip/riser sits on the thumb side of the lifeline. The grip should rest along the thumb bone where it meets the wrist.

My friend and pro shooter John Dudley—a former US national team member—says a great way to check this is to fold your pinky in to where it meets your palm and note that spot. As you draw and aim the bow, you do not want the grip to touch that area of your palm. If it does, you are rotating too deep into the grip and likely to bring your arm in line with the string's path.

It is also important to consciously keep the fingers of your bow hand relaxed throughout the shot cycle. Many archers let their fingers hang loosely off the side of the grip. Some curl their fingers inward and allow their knuckles to rest against the side of the grip, and others lightly curl

Proper bow-hand placement, shown here, keeps contact between the hand and bow riser on the thumb side of the lifeline. This aligns the force of the bow with the bones of your forearm.

If you squeeze the bow grip too tightly while shooting, it will result in an over-rotated grip, as shown here. This not only brings your arm in line with the string's path but also results in sideways torque on the bow riser, which will bring your arrow out of alignment with the target as you release the bowstring.

Facing page: It is important to keep the fingers of your bow hand relaxed while drawing, aiming, and shooting. There are several ways of doing this, as illustrated here. Some archers prefer to let their fingers hang loosely off the side of the grip, others curl their fingers inward and allow their knuckles to rest against the side of the grip, and others just lightly curl their fingers around the grip without squeezing.

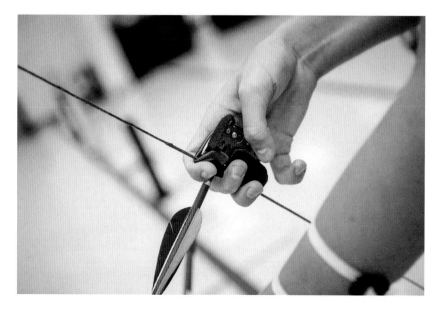

When preparing to shoot a recurve bow, you want to place your fingers on the string and apply just enough pressure to create some light tension as you raise the bow and draw.

their fingers around the riser. Your goal is to find a method that is comfortable for you and prevents you from squeezing the riser in your bow hand and introducing side-to-side torque.

If you are shooting a recurve bow, another important step of the pre-draw is to set your fingers on the string and apply just enough pressure to create some light tension as you raise the bow and prepare to draw. It is important that you have a consistent finger placement on the string, which should be set just behind the first joint of your middle finger. Properly distributing the weight of the bowstring throughout the draw cycle is also important. It is generally recommended to keep 60 percent of the string tension on your middle finger, with 20 percent each on your index and ring fingers.

DRAWING THE BOW

As we discussed in the previous chapter, you should be able to draw the bowstring back in one fluid motion and end up in a perfect T form, with your bow arm level and pointing straight toward the target, your drawing arm level and pointing directly away from the target, and your body in the middle. Again, you want to keep the elbow of your bow arm straight but not hyperextended. Although many archers, including some

This Olympic recurve archer is demonstrating proper bow arm alignment, all the way from the bow hand to the shoulder.

of the very best, prefer to keep a slight bend in the elbow of the bow arm, doing so can cause inconsistency if you don't bend your arm exactly the same way on every shot. Remember, **consistent accuracy** is all about **consistent form,** so stick with a routine that will help you reduce variables and increase consistency. Keeping a straight arm also maintains a biomechanically strong position. One way to understand the benefit of a proper bow grip and arm alignment is to imagine all the energy of the bow being transferred through your thumb bone to the wrist and straight up the bones of the arm to the shoulder. You want to maintain a straight alignment of this skeletal structure so that the bones help support the bow and maintain proper alignment on target.

Another important aspect to good T form is your head position. If you are a compound shooter and your draw length is set properly, the string should stop just past the corner of your mouth and you should be able to touch the tip of your nose to the bowstring as you look through the peep sight. If your draw length is too short, you may have to lean your head forward to meet the string. If your draw length is too long, the string will go well past the corner of your mouth and rest against the side of your nose. You should not have to tilt your head forward or backward to meet the string.

When shooting a compound bow, you should be able to touch the tip of your nose to the bowstring as you look through the peep sight. If your draw length is set too short, you will likely have to crane your head forward to meet the string. Notice how a short draw also prevents your rear elbow from properly aligning with the shot. If your draw length is set too long, the string will go past the corner of your mouth and rest against the side of your face, resulting in erratic string oscillation as it moves past your face upon release. CHRISTIAN BERG PHOTOS

When drawing an Olympic recurve bow, hold your head still, in a natural position, while bringing the bowstring to your face. Your drawing hand should start at roughly eye level as you bring the string back.

Similarly, if you are shooting an Olympic recurve, you should be able to hold your head still in a natural position facing the target as you draw the string to your face. Your drawing hand should start at roughly eye level as you bring the bowstring back to your face and anchoring position.

ANCHORING

Regardless of what type of bow you shoot, the whole point of an "anchor" position is to establish some reference points that allow for consistent hand/string positioning shot after shot. As I have stressed several times, consistency is critical to successful shooting, and finding your ideal position will help achieve that. Because each person's body and equipment setup are different, there will naturally be some variation in anchor points from one archer to the next. However, this section will give you some good guidelines to follow.

Whether you shoot a compound or recurve bow, you want to identify a bone-on-bone anchor reference that allows you to repeat the exact hand placement at full draw shot after shot. The most common anchor point for compound shooters is to place the knuckle at the base of the index finger against the skull at the base of the ear. Traditional shooters will generally anchor their knuckles somewhere along the cheekbone, while Olympic recurve shooters will generally have a lower anchor point

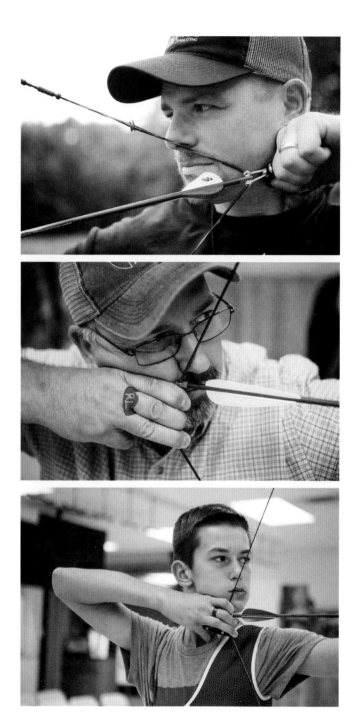

Regardless of what type of bow you shoot, a good anchor point utilizes a bone-on-bone reference point that produces consistent placement shot after shot. These images represent the most common anchor positions for compound, traditional, and Olympic recurve shooters.

along the jawbone. In all cases, however, this bone-on-bone interface provides a solid and reliable reference as a primary anchor point.

In addition to having a primary anchor reference, most archers have one or more secondary references to help them maintain consistency and proper alignment at full draw. For compound shooters, the peep sight serves as the most important secondary reference, as the shooter's head must be properly positioned in relation to the bowstring in order to see through the peep sight and place the sight pin on target. In fact, your peep sight and sight pins serve as rear and front aiming references in much the same way as the iron sights on a rifle. Just as your cheek must be properly aligned on a gunstock in order to aim properly, so too must your face be properly aligned with your bow. Often, a compound shooter will find that his or her dominant eye lines up perfectly with the peep sight just as the tip of the nose touches the bowstring, providing a third anchor point reference. Many compound shooters also choose to add a kisser button to their bowstring for what would be a third or even fourth anchor reference, depending on your shooting style. A kisser button is positioned on the string so that the rubber disc contacts the corner of the shooter's mouth at full draw. When all these reference points are combined— proper hand placement, good peep alignment, and either placing the nose on the bowstring or using a kisser button—they allow an archer to aim and release from the same anchor position shot after shot.

Some compound shooters employ a kisser button to provide an additional reference point that helps ensure a consistent anchor point on every shot.

CHAPTER 8
Advanced Aiming

THIS BOOK CONTAINS A WEALTH OF INFORMATION, but I can't imagine anything will help you more than the information contained in this chapter and the next. If there is a "secret" to successful shooting, I believe this is it.

It is difficult for new shooters to fully understand the importance of aiming and the role back tension plays in creating a surprise release. We'll discuss aiming here and back tension in chapter 9. Understanding these two fundamental concepts—and putting them into practice in your own shooting—will do wonders for your performance. In fact, it was only after many years of shooting that I experienced a breakthrough in understanding that allowed me to shoot with the confidence and consistency I sought. It is my hope that the information included here will speed your learning process and help you avoid some of the difficulties I faced.

AIMING AS A MIND-SET

You will *never* unleash your full potential as an archer until you abandon the idea of consciously controlling the shot. I do not even like the term "shoot," because I do not believe that is my job as an archer. I've taken this concept so far as to tell people that I don't go outside to "shoot" my bow. Rather, I go outside to "aim" my bow. And if I aim well and employ proper back tension, the shooting takes care of itself. Everything changed for the better once I abandoned the notion that aiming is only a precursor to squeezing the trigger and embraced the idea that aiming is a continuous, critical task that requires my total focus throughout the shot cycle and until the arrow hits the target.

As you forge ahead in your own archery journey, I urge you to think about aiming as your most important task. Your bow (regardless of style) is a remarkably reliable machine that will put arrows in the bull's-eye **IF YOU LET IT.** The bow will do the same thing again and again **IF** you do the same thing again and again.

I'd like to again borrow from my friend John Dudley and repeat a little story he likes to share with his archery students. As John explains, the best shots you ever make will be the easiest shots you ever make. And some of the worst shots you ever make will be the hardest. That may sound confusing at first, but John's point is that a truly perfect archery shot will feel

Aiming is a continuous process throughout the shot sequence. You should strive to remain completely focused on the target from the time you reach full draw until your arrow hits home. PHOTO COURTESY OF PETERSEN'S BOWHUNTING

effortless and relaxing. This is what athletes commonly refer to as "being in the zone." Meanwhile, some of the worst shots occur when archers are full of tension and their minds are occupied with so many things they are unable to settle down and just let the bow do its thing.

In terms of aiming, this concept can easily be illustrated when you consider the difference between trying to command the shot at the very moment your sight pin hits the bull's-eye and simply focusing on bringing the pin back to the center of the bull's-eye over and over again as it naturally drifts off center.

As I mentioned in chapter 5, your sight pin will *never* remain perfectly still on the bull's-eye. Our arms and shoulders are not vises we can simply point toward the target and lock into place; movement as we breathe and engage our muscles to aim is perfectly natural, and not even Olympic champions are immune to this. The key is not whether the pin is going to move off target (because it will) but rather how we deal with that mentally.

For many archers, even experienced shooters, the mind is filled with anxiety over the inability to keep the sight pin exactly where you want it to be all the time. A natural outcome of such a mind-set is to anticipate the pin's path at it moves up, down, left, and right and succumb to the temptation to consciously time the release of the arrow at the instant the pin hits the intended target. The result is inconsistent shooting and a host of other problems, as we'll discuss more in the next chapter.

Conversely, archers who accept the fact that the sight pin will move continuously will not be stressed out over trying to hold it still. Instead, they will simply continue to aim to the best of their ability, bringing the pin back as close to center as they can over and over again as they remain

You are not a robot, and your sight pin will never hold completely still while you're aiming. Do not allow yourself to become anxious about this natural movement. Instead, simply concentrate on the spot you want to hit and gently guide your pin back on target when it drifts. PHOTO COURTESY OF PETERSEN'S BOWHUNTING

focused on their intended point of impact and maintain good shooting form as they wait for the shot to happen. This mind-set allows the shooter to remain relaxed throughout the shot process and is very conducive to successful shooting.

THE PRACTICAL APPLICATION

What does this notion of "aiming" instead of "shooting" look like as a practical matter? It really boils down to viewing the act of aiming as an ongoing process rather than a single moment in time.

As you draw the bow and settle into your anchor position, bring your sight pin on target and simply do your best to bring it back to center as it naturally drifts. If you are shooting a compound bow with a multi-pin bow sight, center the round pin guard on your sight inside the round peep sight aperture rather than centering the sight pin you are using. This will result in a consistent anchor point regardless of shot distance and will produce consistent accuracy.

If you are shooting an Olympic recurve, place the pin on target and bring it back to center over and over again as it drifts, keeping your string just outside the pin housing as a reference for proper alignment. Simply

When looking through your peep sight, try to keep the round pin guard on your bow sight centered with your peep sight rather than centering the particular pin you are using to aim on that shot. This will result in a more consistent anchor point regardless of shot distance and will produce consistent accuracy. PHOTO COURTESY OF PETERSEN'S BOWHUNTING

continue aiming, and keep total focus on your target as you gradually increase tension on your bowstring and wait for the clicker to sound.

In either case, the key is to remain as relaxed as possible and allow your subconscious mind to continue aiming until the arrow is released and hits the target, which will result in a clean release and good follow-through. If you find that your conscious mind is preoccupied with a desire to hold the pin in place and/or an overwhelming urge to squeeze the trigger or release the string at the exact instant the pin passes over the center of the bull's-eye, you are setting yourself up for failure.

Now let's take a look at the importance of back tension and a surprise release to see exactly how good aiming habits translate directly into good shooting.

CHAPTER 9

Back Tension and the Surprise Release

THE IDEA OF USING BACK TENSION TO CREATE A SURPRISE RELEASE builds directly on the foundation of aiming as a continuous mind-set. For many archers, especially new ones, the concept of a "surprise" shot is difficult to understand. After all, when you draw and aim your bow, you know the shot is soon to follow, right? While this is indeed true, I assure you there is a world of difference between consciously commanding your arrow's release and employing back tension to create an effortless release that is so fluid and natural it will literally take you by surprise—even though you "knew" it was coming.

Back tension is so critical to unlocking an archer's full potential that it is the release method used by all the world's top target shooters. Unfortunately, despite its importance, relatively few shooters fully understand how to generate proper back tension and what a true surprise release feels like.

BACK TENSION DEFINED

Simply put, back tension is using the muscles of the back to maintain a *dynamic* pull on the bowstring at full draw that results in an *unanticipated* shot. Again, this method stands in stark contrast to a *static* pull on the bowstring at full draw and a *commanded* shot.

You can get a pretty good idea of whether an archer is utilizing back tension simply by watching them shoot. If, upon release of the arrow, the drawing arm and bow arm remain relatively still, chances are back tension was not employed. Instead, the shooter was probably using a static pull. When I watch compound bow shooters who consciously command the shot, typically the only movement I will see at the shot is their index finger squeezing the trigger on the release aid. Recurve shooters will similarly be rigid, with only their fingers relaxing to release the bowstring.

On the other hand, archers who properly employ back tension will experience noticeable movement upon releasing the arrow. Because an archer using back tension is applying continually increasing backward

These photos show the difference between a static (top) and dynamic (bottom) release. Consciously releasing the arrow results in a static release, while properly employing back tension and allowing the shot to happen naturally results in a dynamic release that will cause your bow hand to jump forward and your release hand to jump backward at the moment the string is released.

pressure to the bowstring, the drawing elbow will jump backward away from the target at the moment the string is released. And the bow arm will simultaneously move out toward the target as tension is relieved.

WHAT BACK TENSION FEELS LIKE

To help you understand what back tension feels like on a practical level, I am again going to share an exercise John Dudley uses with his own students. Here goes:

Step 1: Start out by standing with your arms at your side; then raise your arms straight up to shoulder height, with your thumbs pointing up.

Step 2: Next, bend the elbow of your drawing arm so that your release hand comes toward the body and your fingertips touch the center of your chest.

Step 3: Look back at your bent elbow and imagine it as being pointed as the 12 on a clock dial. Next, try moving the elbow back to the two o'clock position (if you are a right-handed shooter) or the ten o'clock position (if you are a left-handed shooter). This should cause your fingers to slide 2 or 3 inches away from the center of your chest.

Repeat this process several times, starting with your hands at your side, raising your arms and then bringing your release hand to your chest and moving your elbow inward toward your back.

CHRISTIAN BERG PHOTOS

As you do, you will feel muscles tightening between the spine and your shoulder blade. These are the rhomboid muscles, and they are responsible for retracting the scapula. They are also the muscles you need to use in order to properly release your arrow using back tension. Now let's talk about how to properly use that motion in tandem with your release aid (compound shooters) or release hand (Olympic recurve shooters).

EXECUTING A SURPRISE RELEASE

When learning to execute your shot routine using back tension to create a surprise release, it is critical to focus on the process and ignore the result. This is best learned by shooting a blank target face (no bull's-eye or other aiming point) from very close range. This is a common training exercise in archery known as "blank bale shooting," and it allows you to focus completely on your back tension and how the whole process feels without worrying about arrow placement.

Compound Shooters

For the purpose of this segment, I am going to assume you are shooting with an index-finger, wrist-strap release aid. The first thing you want to do, if your release allows it, is to adjust the travel on your trigger so there is as little movement as possible before the release's hook or jaws open. Just as with the trigger on a firearm, you want the trigger on your archery release to be as crisp as possible. If you can also adjust trigger tension, you want it set just heavy enough so that you can confidently wrap your index finger around it without releasing the bowstring.

Once your release is properly calibrated, put it on and start your normal shot routine. Raise your bow arm, come to full draw, find your anchor point, and center your pin guard inside your peep sight. Next, place your pin on the blank target and allow it to float freely. Again, do *not* put the emphasis on aiming here.

Now take your index finger and wrap it completely around the trigger, forming the shape of a hook, where the trigger is located on the second pad of your index finger between the first and second joints. Your fingertips are very sensitive, and it is very difficult to avoid the temptation to control trigger pressure with them. We avoid that by keeping our fingertips off the trigger completely.

With your finger curled completely around the trigger, build slight pressure on the trigger but do not continue squeezing. Now gently relax the other fingers on your release hand so that the weight of the bowstring is focused solely on your wrist, the release strap, and the release head.

Finally, with your finger still curled around the trigger, focus on pulling your rear elbow toward an object directly behind you, engaging the rhomboid muscles as you did in the previous exercise. At the same time, think about using your bow hand to push directly toward the target, being aware of this "push-pull" tension the bowstring is creating between your forward-facing bow hand and rearward-facing back elbow. Now gradually increase tension in your rhomboid muscles until your scapula

When shooting an index-finger release aid, it is best to wrap the finger completely around the trigger rather than firing the trigger with your fingertip.
JOHN DUDLEY/NOCK ON ARCHERY PHOTO

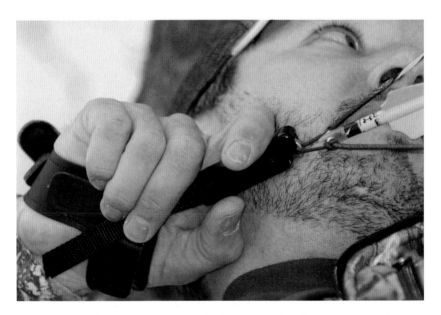

When using an index-finger release aid, keep the other fingers of your release hand relaxed and allow all the tension of the bowstring to be taken up by the release. JOHN DUDLEY/NOCK ON ARCHERY PHOTO

When using back to tension to fire your shot, you should feel tension build as you push toward the target with your bow arm and pull away from the target with your release arm. JOHN DUDLEY/NOCK ON ARCHERY PHOTO

retracts in toward the middle of your back, creating enough movement in your arm to cause the release to open and the bowstring to shoot forward *without* having to move your index finger. As tension builds, you should feel it in both your bow arm and release arm as you gradually pull harder against the bow's built-in draw stops that contact the limbs and/or cables. At the shot, the elbow of your release arm should fly backward while your bow arm moves forward toward the target.

When done properly, the exact moment of the bowstring's release should take you by surprise, even though your conscious mind knows the shot is imminent. Repeat this process over and over again, keeping your thoughts focused solely on the tension building in your rhomboid muscles and the tension on your trigger slowly increasing as you allow the pin to float naturally on the target.

If you are attempting to follow these instructions but simply can't seem to fire the release, gradually adjust the trigger tension downward and repeat the process until it works.

Olympic Recurve Shooters

The muscles used and the process of creating back tension are the same regardless of whether you shoot a compound or recurve bow. However, the practical application differs slightly between the two.

Because there is no set draw length on a recurve bow, it is critical that the same draw length be used on each shot; otherwise, the poundage pulled and energy stored will vary from arrow to arrow. That is one of the big reasons Olympic recurve shooters use a clicker, which makes an audible sound at the instant the optimal draw length is reached, prompting the archer to release the string.

By employing a clicker, Olympic recurve shooters are able to focus intently on aiming as they complete the final stage of the drawing process and release the arrow at the moment the clicker sounds.

BACK-TENSION RELEASE AIDS

Although you can properly use back tension to trigger the shot with any kind of release aid, many archers find it helpful to use a back-tension release aid to help them learn the proper technique. As the name implies, a back-tension release aid is a release that is activated via back tension. There is no trigger to fire the shot; rather, the string is released when sufficient back tension is achieved.

Back-tension releases are generally handheld designs and come in two styles: hinge-style and tension-activated releases. A hinge release uses a pivoting string hook that requires the shooter to build back tension in order to rotate the hook to the release point. A tension-activated release simply activates when a preset amount of tension is applied to the string at full draw. A manual safety, typically engaged by the thumb, is held while drawing and anchoring; once the archer

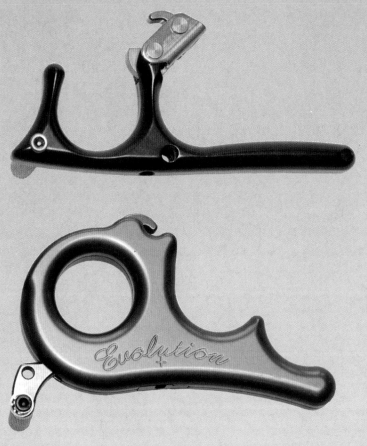

Back-tension release aids are available in two basic styles: hinge-style (top) and tension-activated (bottom) releases. PHOTOS COURTESY OF CARTER ENTERPRISES

is settled on target, the safety is disengaged and the shooter simply continues aiming and building back tension until the shot fires.

If you are a compound shooter who is serious about learning how to properly execute shots using a surprise release—and you should be—I highly encourage you to try both styles of back-tension releases at your local pro shop and purchase the one that feels most comfortable to you. Back-tension releases are not just great training aids for learning how to properly employ back tension; they are widely used by many of the world's top professional archers in competition because they are so helpful in maintaining proper shooting form.

Several years ago, after struggling with a variety of shooting problems, I began using back-tension releases to help reprogram my mind and break bad habits. I was so impressed with how helpful these releases were to my form that I made a permanent switch and now do all my shooting, both on the practice range and on my hunts, using a Carter Evolution tension-activated release. The biggest benefit of using a back-tension release is that it completely eliminates the need for the archer to physically squeeze a trigger in order to shoot. Rather, it frees your mind to focus completely on aiming and building back tension as you remain focused on the target and wait for the shot to fire.

Author Christian Berg uses a Carter Evolution tension-activated release for all his shooting, both on the target range and in the field. Berg used the release on this successful deer hunt in South Dakota. CHRISTIAN BERG PHOTO

But while the clicker plays a key role in ensuring draw length is properly calibrated on each shot, it also plays a critical role in helping archers use proper back tension. Typically, an Olympic recurve shooter is going to reach his or her anchor position roughly a quarter to half an inch of draw away from activating the clicker. So rather than using a static draw in which the string is drawn to the optimal position and held there while aiming, the archer is instead able to anchor, place the pin on target, and allow the pin to float and aim continually as the string continues to be drawn that extra little bit until the clicker is activated and the arrow is released. It is during these final few seconds before the shot that the Olympic recurve archer is able to focus completely on aiming and gradually increasing string tension until the clicker is activated and the string is released.

WHY BACK TENSION IS SO CRITICAL

You will never achieve your full potential as an archer until you learn to adopt aiming as a mind-set and execute your shots using back tension. By this point, you should have a good understanding of how these two concepts work together to create the perfect archery shot. However, I am sure at least some of you are still wondering, "Do I *really* need to shoot this way? After all, the way I'm doing it now seems to work just fine."

I'm not going to deny that it is entirely possible to shoot quite well by commanding your shot. In fact, there are many good recreational shooters who consciously command their shots, and even a few professional shooters manage to get by with it. However, it is very, very difficult, if not impossible, to shoot well over the long term this way. The reason is that, sooner or later, you are going to experience one or more problems collectively referred to in the archery world as "target panic."

Target panic gets its name because it is caused by anxiety over placing your pin on target. Archers who suffer from target panic may not perceive this anxiety as a full-fledged "panic," but there is definitely a mental stress associated with it. Target panic manifests in a multitude of ways, but the common theme is an intense desire to release the arrow before proper aim is achieved. Two of the most common symptoms are punching the trigger and a physical inability to place the sight pin on the bull's-eye.

As a new shooter, it may be difficult for you to imagine not being able to draw and place your pin on the target; but as someone who has suffered from severe target panic, I can tell you that, at its worst, it is almost as though there is a physical force preventing you from placing your sight pin where you want it. In my case, I had a tendency to "freeze" below the bull's-eye, and no matter how much I tried, I literally could not raise my bow arm to place the pin in the right spot. This caused so much anxiety (panic) during my shooting sessions that I would forcibly jerk my bow arm up and hammer the trigger on my release aid at the same time in an attempt to time the shot at the exact moment the pin swung through the bull's-eye. This is a common response to target panic known as "drive-by" shooting, and I can tell you that I've sailed more than a few good arrows into the woods beyond my backyard target doing it. After battling increasingly troublesome target panic for several years, I was, thankfully, able to overcome it and restore my shooting confidence with the help of back-tension release aids and sound advice from fellow archers who had battled similar demons.

Although a deeper discussion of target panic—and how to overcome it—is beyond the scope of this book, I've shared this much to make a simple point: Don't be like me! Build good habits from the start. Make your focus on aiming, not shooting, and learn how to release your arrows via back tension. Committing to this now will save you lots of headaches later.

CHAPTER 10

Why You Missed (and How to Fix It)

YOU WILL NOTICE A SIGNIFICANT BOOST IN YOUR CONFIDENCE as you develop your shot routine and refine your form by applying the principles and techniques we've discussed so far. Before long, you will be able to consistently group arrows around the bull's-eye at 20, 30, and even 40 yards. As you improve, however, you are likely to encounter occasional struggles and days when it just seems as though your arrows aren't going where you want. During such times, the million-dollar question becomes, "Why did I miss?"

The good news is that even though we all miss the mark from time to time, most problems are the result of small breakdowns in form that are easily corrected. And as you gain experience as a shooter and more familiarity with your personal shooting style, you will get better at recognizing your flaws and getting yourself back on track. In fact, the ability to recognize an error and correct it after only a few shots—instead of a few dozen or a few hundred—is one of the big skills that separates world-class archers from the rest of us. Although it would be impossible to cover every possible archery mistake and how to correct it in this chapter, we will take a look at some of the most common causes of errant shots and how to eliminate them.

EQUIPMENT PROBLEMS

Even a minor equipment issue can cause major accuracy problems. For example, a setscrew that comes loose on your arrow rest can result in steering your arrows far off course. Similarly, a loose screw on your sight can allow your pin to move well off target, resulting in arrows that may not only miss the mark but miss the target entirely. Once you have your bow and accessories properly tuned, it's a good idea to make sure all screws and adjustment knobs are tightly secured. Many archers like to use a dab of thread-locking gel such as Loctite to prevent critical adjustment points from rattling loose. It can also be very helpful to use a pencil to

You can avoid many potential equipment issues by locking your setscrews in place with thread-locking gel and using a pencil to mark the proper settings of your arrow rest and sight so that you can easily tell if they've moved out of place.

Examine your bow regularly for signs of wear, such as frayed or loose serving thread. This is an extreme example, but even minor serving problems can cause big problems. If you discover a problem, don't continue shooting the bow. Instead, visit your local pro shop for needed repairs.

visibly mark the proper location of your arrow rest, bow sight, and sight pins. That makes it easy to inspect your bow before each shooting session to ensure everything is in its proper place.

In addition to being familiar with your bow settings, you should inspect your bow for physical damage and obvious wear before each use. Strings and cables can stretch over time, which can have a significant effect on the impact point of your arrows. Worn center serving can result in erratic nock releases. A frayed or loose peep sight serving can allow your peep sight to "migrate" in your string, resulting in a change to your anchor point and sight alignment.

When you encounter a problem with your shooting and aren't sure what the cause is, a good first step is to thoroughly examine your equipment for problems. However, if everything appears to be in good working order, I want to caution you against "chasing" the bull's-eye by moving your sight pin. Because while equipment issues can certainly throw your arrows off target, it is **much** more likely that you have changed something about the way you are shooting. In fact, it is fairly common for small changes in your form to result in a slightly different arrow impact point from day to day, even though your equipment is exactly the same. We'll spend the rest of this chapter looking at some common shooting flaws and how to correct them.

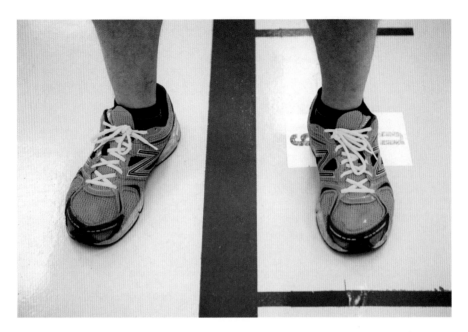

Use a reference line to ensure that you are maintaining a consistent stance from shot to shot and day to day. If you shoot outdoors, you can simply scratch a reference line in the dirt.

INCONSISTENT STANCE

Your stance serves as the foundation of your shooting platform and also determines your body's orientation to the target. You must use a consistent stance, as any variation from shot to shot will affect your accuracy. If you haven't already completed the exercise outlined in chapter 6 on how to find your ideal stance, now is a good time to revisit that. Once you've found your ideal stance, make sure to repeat it on every shot. Placing tape on the floor as a reference can help you assume the same foot position time after time until it becomes automatic.

INCONSISTENT ANCHOR OR TOO MUCH FACIAL PRESSURE

As with your stance, your anchor position must be repeated shot after shot in order to shoot with consistent accuracy. Even slight changes in your anchor point will change the relationship between your face, the bowstring, and your peep sight and/or sight pin.

In addition to having a consistent anchor point, you want to develop an anchor point that results in minimal contact between your face and bowstring and/or arrow. Ideally, the tip of your nose will only lightly

These photos show an archer applying too much facial pressure to the bowstring and an acceptable amount of pressure to the bowstring. Excessive contact between the string and your face can induce sideways torque on the string upon release, resulting in poor accuracy.

touch the string at full draw, and pressure between the face and bowstring will be slight. If you anchor your drawing hand in deep behind your ear, it is easy to press the bowstring or arrow nock hard against your cheek, and this friction will result in sideways string oscillation upon release, causing erratic arrow flight. Even a little bit of added facial pressure is enough to move your arrow from the bull's-eye to a near miss. You also want to watch the amount of pressure you apply to the bowstring with your nose. You should not barely touch the string with your nose on one shot and then have the string squishing your nose on the next. Focus on doing everything the same way every time, and keep facial pressure to a minimum for the cleanest arrow release possible.

POOR GRIP AND BOW TORQUE

An improper grip and the associated bow torque is one of the most common archery mistakes—and something done by every shooter at one time or another. As previously discussed, you never want to "grip" your bow grip. Rather, your hand should remain relaxed throughout the shot cycle, with the bow riser resting freely in the V-shaped notch between your thumb and index finger. However, many archers tend to clench the grip more tightly when they feel pressure; this results in side-to-side torque on the bow and inconsistent left and right arrow groupings.

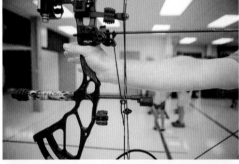

Another common problem is that many archers subconsciously grab at the riser immediately upon release of the arrow. If you are not using proper back tension to achieve a surprise arrow release, it is easy to do this without even thinking

This series of images illustrate a good, relaxed bow grip; an over-rotated hand creating bow torque; and an overly tight grip on the handle creating bow torque.

about it. What happens when you consciously command the shot is that you cannot prevent your bow hand from knowing what your release hand is doing. As a result, the brain sends a signal to your bow hand to grab the riser at the very instant your release hand is triggering the shot. The result is a quick burst of sideways bow torque as the arrow leaves the bow, typically manifesting itself in misses to the left for right-handed shooters and misses to the right for left-handed shooters. If you start missing off to the side for no apparent reason, take a second look at your grip, and focus on maintaining that relaxed, torque-free interface with the bow all the way until your arrow hits the target.

PLUCKED STRING

Plucking the string is another way to introduce sideways torque on the bowstring at the moment of release. Whether you are shooting a compound or a recurve bow, you should release the string cleanly and your bow arm should move directly backward, away from the string. However, if you pull your hand sideways, away from your face, as you release the string, you will pluck the string like a guitar as it begins to move forward. This will cause the string to oscillate side to side as the arrow is launched, again resulting in poor arrow flight and inconsistent left/right impact.

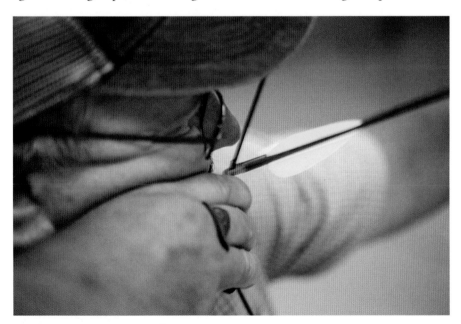

Plucking the string, or pulling the bowstring away from your face at the moment of release, introduces sideways torque on the string and results in poor accuracy.

POOR FOLLOW-THROUGH

Although there can be many reasons for an errant shot, I believe poor follow-through is responsible for as many misses as any other reason. This is true for a couple reasons. First, virtually all archers—even those with lots of experience—struggle with their follow-through from time to time. Second, poor follow-through can manifest in a variety of ways.

As we have already discussed, follow-through is extremely important to accuracy because any small mistakes you make as the arrow is leaving the bow can throw your arrow off course, even if just slightly, resulting in an impact point that misses the mark. If you find yourself suddenly missing shots for no apparent reason, I encourage you to take a few deep breaths and shoot another group while focusing carefully on maintaining good form throughout the shot and holding both your head and bow arm steady still until the arrow hits the target.

Perhaps the most common issue that impacts follow-through is dropping the bow arm at the instant the arrow is released. Personally, I find this issue can become particularly troublesome during long shooting sessions when the shoulder of the bow arm becomes fatigued from holding the bow up over the course of many shots. As a result of that fatigue, there is a natural desire to lower the bow as quickly as possible once the arrow

Dropping the bow arm upon release is a common flaw in follow-through that results in misses that are low and left for right-handed archers and low and right for left-handed archers.

When shooting, try to avoid the temptation to "peek," or quickly move your bow out of the way in an effort to better watch the arrow in flight. This quick movement of the bow just after releasing the string typically results in poor arrow flight.

is gone. If you aren't careful to hold the bow steady until the arrow hits the target, doing this will result in misses that are low and left for right-handed archers and low and right for lefties.

Another common follow-through problem is what's known as "peeking." This happens when, due to an overwhelming desire to watch your arrow in flight, you move your head away from the bowstring and/or your bow out of your line of sight at the moment the string is released. Not surprisingly, this sudden motion, with your head moving in one direction and your bow moving in another, is not conducive to accurate shots. Thankfully, it is fairly easy to watch your arrow in flight without peeking, so simply maintain your form and hold steady until the arrow hits the target.

Yet another problem that can cause poor follow-through is flinching, or physically jerking your body at the moment of the shot. Flinching typically occurs with shooters who consciously command the shot rather than using the preferred method of executing a surprise release by building back tension. When consciously commanding the shot, it is impossible for your mind not to anticipate this action, and any anxiety about the process can manifest itself in a sudden jerk or shudder just as the arrow is leaving the bow. Again, this throws off your aim at the worst possible time and can result in an arrow that not only misses the bull's-eye but possibly the entire target.

The good news is that problems with follow-through, although common, are relatively easy to fix. If you think you may be suffering from poor follow-through, one of the easiest ways to diagnose the problem is to have a fellow shooter watch as you release the arrow and then point out any unwanted movement. A video camera can be a great tool here as well, allowing you to record your shot routine and identify any issues on screen. With the exception of flinching, which may require an extended period of retraining using back tension to create a surprise release, most other issues associated with poor follow-through can be addressed simply by identifying the problem and then making a focused effort to eliminate it on the range. In fact, it is not unusual for archers to see an immediate improvement in their accuracy once a follow-through problem has been properly identified and corrected.

CHAPTER 11
Archery Games for Family Fun

There are many archery games you can play with friends and family, and they are a great way to have a good time and hone your shooting skills in the process.

WE'VE JUST SPENT A GOOD DEAL OF TIME DISCUSSING THE FINER POINTS OF SHOOTING, and I certainly hope you've found it helpful. However, I also recognize the reason we all took up archery in the first place is because we just wanted to have fun—and *that* is what this chapter is all about!

While the challenge of hitting the bull's-eye is certainly enjoyable, it's also exciting to try new and different things. Variety is the spice of life, after all, and incorporating games into your shooting routine will help keep you fresh and provide new ways to refocus your mind on the importance of accuracy. Using games is an excellent way to hold the interest of younger shooters and maintain their enthusiasm for archery long after the novelty of simply shooting a bow has worn off. Plus, it's just a lot of fun for the whole family and a good excuse to head into the backyard and spend some quality time together.

With that in mind, this chapter provides instruction on a number of archery games you and your family can enjoy together. There are literally hundreds of archery games out there, so this chapter is by no means an exhaustive list. However, the activities presented here were chosen because they are appropriate for all ages, relatively easy to set up, and don't require any major financial investments.

BOWLING

This creative take on bowling is a lot of fun and will help reinforce the importance of proper shot placement. All you'll need is a cardboard box and ten paper cups to play. Use the box as a platform to position the cups directly in front of your archery target, and build the cups into a pyramid with four cups on the base level, three cups on level two, two cups on level three, and one cup at the top.

Archery bowling is a simple variant on the actual game. Simply use ten paper or plastic cups to set up your "pins" in front of an archery target.

How to play: Each archer gets two arrows per turn. The goal is to knock over as many cups as possible with the first arrow and then knock over any remaining cups with the second arrow. Any cups knocked off or shot through count as 1 point. Any cup that falls onto a cup below it and remains stacked also counts as 1 point. A miss is treated as a gutter ball and worth 0 points. Simply tally each archer's total score for a predetermined number of frames to determine the overall winner. A typical round of bowling consists of ten frames, but you can play five frames or any other number you wish.

HORSESHOES

This game is modeled after the popular backyard picnic game. You can easily create your own archery horseshoe targets with some markers and large pieces of paper. Simply draw an upright horseshoe on the paper and then draw a circle at its inside base to represent the metal post the horseshoes are thrown at. For beginning archers, you can make the horseshoe large and wide; for more experienced shooters, make the horseshoe smaller and narrower. Once drawn, simply affix the paper to the front of your regular archery target with tape or target pins.

How to play: Each player gets three arrows per turn. Arrows that hit the horseshoe are worth 1 point, arrows that land inside the horseshoe

Horseshoes is an easy game for beginning archers to play, and the size of the target area can easily be made large enough for archers of any skill level to be successful.

are worth 2 points, and arrows that hit the metal post count as a "ringer" and are worth 3 points. Any arrows that land outside the horseshoe score a 0. Either give each shooter an equal number of turns and then declare the person with the highest score the winner or play to a certain score, such as 15, and declare the first player to accumulate 15 points the winner.

FOLLOW THE ARROW

This game is modeled after the popular basketball game of H–O–R–S–E, in which shooters must match a shot made by another player. The archery version is played on a standard five-color competition target face.

How to play: Flip a coin or use some other random method to determine the players' shooting order. The first archer shoots an arrow anywhere into the target, and each subsequent archer must shoot an

BREAKOUT BOX: EXPLORE ARCHERY

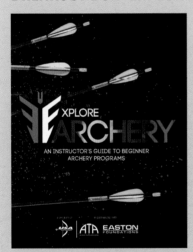

PHOTO COURTESY OF THE ARCHERY TRADE ASSOCIATION

The first four games in this chapter were adapted with permission from the Explore Archery curriculum developed by USA Archery in partnership with the Archery Trade Association and Easton Foundations. Designed especially for new and beginning archers, Explore Archery includes fun, fast-paced programs ranging in length from a couple hours to six weeks. Explore Archery programs are taught by certified USA Archery instructors and cover important skills such as safety and proper shooting form. Students also get to play a variety of exciting games and earn achievement awards that recognize their newfound talents.

Explore Archery programs are hosted by parks and recreation departments, community-based organizations, state parks, archery retailers, and other groups across the nation. To learn more about Explore Archery and find a local program in your area, visit the "Find It" section of the USA Archery website at teamusa.org/USA-Archery/programs.

arrow into the same color on the target (but not in exactly the same place as the first shooter's arrow). If an archer fails to hit the same color as the shot being followed, that shooter gets a letter "H." If all archers hit the proper color, the first archer must shoot a second arrow into that color to avoid getting an "H" of his or her own. In subsequent rounds, other archers each get a turn leading off, forcing other shooters to follow the color of their arrow. The game continues until all players except one have spelled "H-O-R-S-E," with the lone remaining shooter the winner.

INSIDE THE RINGS

For this activity, you'll need a pack of long, thin balloons—the kind used to make balloon animals. Ideally, you want to find a multicolor pack that has all five colors in the Olympic rings—blue, yellow, black, green, and red. Blow up one of each color (use different colors if that's what you have), tie the ends together to make a loop, and then pin each balloon loop to the face of your archery target in an overlapping fashion to create the pattern of the interlocking Olympic rings.

How to play: Start out with six arrows for each archer. Shoot at the target with the goal of placing one arrow inside each ring without popping any rings. The first shooter to get an arrow inside each ring, or the one with an arrow inside the most rings, is the winner.

BALLOON EXPLOSION

If there's one certainty in archery, it is that children (of all ages) absolutely LOVE popping balloons with their arrows. Simply blowing up a bunch of balloons, pinning them to your target face, and allowing your kids to shoot until all the balloons are popped is certain to generate plenty of smiles and laughter. However, if you want to kick the balloon game up a couple notches, you can fill your balloons with colored water, glitter, or cornstarch to create a variety of different "explosion" effects upon impact. Simply use a squirt bottle such as those used for ketchup and mustard to get the glitter or cornstarch into the balloons before blowing them up.

How to play: This one is pretty self-explanatory; once you have your customized balloons set up, you just shoot them! You can turn this into a more competitive game by targeting certain balloon colors or assigning different point values to balloons filled with different materials.

Another fun way to enhance this activity—and relive the excitement—is to set up a GoPro or other video camera near the target and capture the impact of the arrows as they pop the balloons. Balloons filled

Balloon Explosion is a simple yet highly visually game guaranteed to hold shooters' attention!

with colored water or glitter create very colorful explosions, while balloons filled with cornstarch seem to disappear in a cloud of smoke.

Note: This activity can cause a bit of a mess, depending on what you place inside the balloons. So keep that in mind when choosing a shooting area and deciding how close to place the balloons in front of your target. If you want to avoid getting corn starch, glitter, or food coloring all over your target face, hang the balloons from a piece of twine strung a foot or two in front of the actual target.

TIC-TAC-TOE

The archery variation of the classic game is easy to set up and fun to play. Simply use painter's tape to create the classic 3 × 3 tic-tac-toe grid on your target face.

How to play: Let two shooters (or two teams of archers) face off until one side has three arrows in a row horizontally, vertically, or

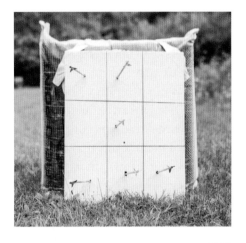

Tic-Tac-Toe is an easy archery game to play. You can increase the challenge simply by increasing the distance from the target.

diagonally. Arrows must be completely within the desired grid space to count, and any shots that touch the tape are considered a miss. If the grid is filled before either side wins, the game is a tie and a new game begins.

FOUR IN A ROW

Modeled after the classic Connect 4 game from Hasbro, this game is similar to tic-tac-toe except it is played on a larger grid that requires more thought and strategy—and more accuracy! Again, you can use painter's tape to create a grid on your target face. You can choose the size of the grid, but a 10 × 10 design allows for fairly intricate game play and also makes the squares small enough that making the shots can be challenging for shooters with advancing skills.

How to play: As the name implies, the object of the game is to get four arrows in a row horizontally, vertically, or diagonally. If the entire grid gets filled before either side wins, the game is a tie and a new game begins. Because the grid for this game is significantly larger than for tic-tac-toe, colored stickers may be helpful for marking each player's hits on the board after arrows are retrieved for additional shooting.

SPLIT THE ARROW

In archery, splitting one arrow with another is considered quite a feat of marksmanship. In fact, the term most commonly used to describe such a

Split the Arrow is a fun game that requires archers to take accuracy and shot angle into consideration in order to be successful.

shot is a "Robin Hood." In this game, you simply take the cardboard tube from a used roll of paper towels and use it as the "arrow" for others to split. You can use the plain tube or, if you prefer, decorate it with colored construction paper and add paper vanes to make it more realistic. Either way, once your cardboard "arrow" is ready, you simply affix it to your target by sticking an arrow into the target face and hanging the cardboard tube on it.

How to play: The goal is to shoot an arrow that goes completely inside the tube. Shots that hit the outside of the tube and punch through to the inside are considered near misses. Remember to adjust the height of the tube so that each shooter can shoot directly into it. You can also increase or decrease the challenge by adjusting the distance of the shot and/or experimenting with different size tubes.

FIND IT

This is a very simple and fun game that is great for younger children and very new shooters because each archer is likely to "hit" multiple shots and have a great chance of winning prizes. Simply use a stack of blank index cards and place a sticker or other picture of what the archers are looking for on one or more of the cards. You can make up any kind of story you want as a narrative for this game to further engage the participants. For example, you could make up a story about rescuing a princess and place knight stickers on nineteen cards and a princess sticker on one card. Then you simply pin all twenty index cards, face down, on the target face to set up the game board.

How to play: Each archer takes a turn shooting the target and revealing the picture behind the card. In the example above, the game continues until one archer hits the card with the princess on the back and is declared the winner. You can offer a prize to the winner and vary the game any way you wish. For example, you could easily have more than one "winning" card on the target face. In fact, the more winning cards—and the more prizes available—the more excited young shooters will be to play. Even small prizes such as a piece of candy, plastic animal figures, pencils, etc., will be enthusiastically received and reinforce positive feelings associated with good shooting.

POKER AND BLACKJACK

In addition to simple games you can set up on your own, there are a variety of popular archery games available on preprinted target faces and/or custom targets. Poker and blackjack are two of the most common and

The Deck of Cards XL from Arrowmat allows archers to play poker, blackjack, and other popular card games with their bow and arrows. PHOTO COURTESY OF ARROWMAT

are easily played using a target face such as the Deck of Cards XL from Arrowmat (arrowmat.com), which features an entire deck of cards.

How to play: Popular games such as five-card stud and blackjack can be played very similar to the real thing. For five-card stud, each shooter is given five arrows to make the best shots possible, with the winner the one who ends up with the best hand. Blackjack could be played the same way, with each player given up to five shots to accumulate the hand equal to or closest to 21 without going bust.

DARTS

Arrowmat also makes a Dartboard target face that allows you to play any game typically played on a regulation dartboard with your bow and arrows. There are literally dozens of games you can play on a dartboard, and a quick Internet search will reveal rules for many of them. Below, I'll provide a brief overview of the most common dart game.

How to play: The most common dart game involves players starting with a score—typically 501 or 301—and counting down to 0. Each player shoots three arrows per turn, with his or her score reduced by the total point value of the arrows shot. Arrows that hit the narrow band on the outer edge of the board are worth double the listed value of that section, while arrows that hit the narrow band closer to the center are worth triple the listed value. Arrows that land in either of the larger sections

The Dartboard target from Arrowmat allows archers to play with arrows instead of darts. PHOTO COURTESY OF ARROWMAT

are worth the listed value for that section. Arrows that hit the center of the board are worth 25 points for the green outer ring and 50 points for the inner bull's-eye. Any arrows that hit the edge of the board where the numbers are printed or anywhere outside the board entirely are worth 0.

The game continues until one player reduces his or her score to 0. However, the final shot that reduces a player's score to 0 *must* be made by hitting a double scoring section. Any shot that reduces a player's score to 0 but does not hit in a double scoring section is considered a "bust"; that player's score reverts to where it was at the start of that turn, and any remaining arrows for that turn are forfeited. Similarly, any shots that reduce a player's score to exactly 1 or below 0 are also considered busts.

BASEBALL AND GOLF

Finally, I wanted to mention two other popular pastimes—golf and baseball—that have loyal archery followings. Perhaps the most popular archery targets made for these games are produced by Morrell Manufacturing Inc. (morrelltargets.com).

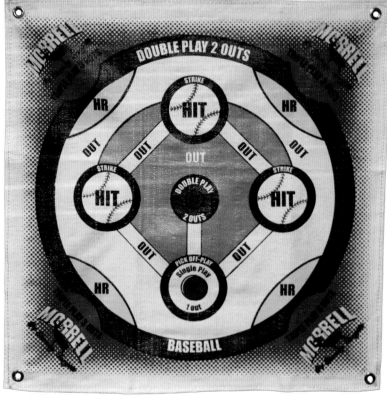

PHOTO COURTESY OF MORRELL TARGETS

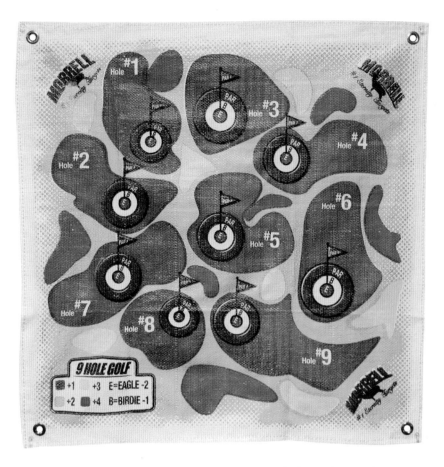

The Baseball and Golf specialty targets from Morrell give archers a chance to put their own twist on these popular ball sports. PHOTO COURTESY OF MORRELL TARGETS

How to play: Game play for these two targets is pretty self-explanatory. In baseball, each player is allowed to "hit" by shooting and accumulating as many runs as possible before three outs are recorded. As you can see from looking at the target, the game face resembles a baseball diamond. Areas for singles are relatively large and surrounded by a ring that only gives the batter a strike. Areas for home runs, however, are surrounded by hazards that could result in a double or even triple play if the shot is missed. So there is a bit of strategy involved as a shooter evaluates the options relative to his or her skills and the risk-versus-reward ratio. Players can decide how many innings they wish to play, with the shooter who has the most total runs at that point declared the winner.

Game play for golf is similar, with the target face representing a nine-hole course. Each archer gets one shot for each hole, scoring either an eagle (2 under par), birdie (1 under par), or par, depending on where he or she hits the circles around each pin. Shots that miss these target areas are penalized, with shots in the fairway counted as 1 over par, shots that land in the rough counted as 2 over par, shots that land in sand traps counted as 3 over par, and shots that land in water counted as 4 over par. After all nine holes have been played, the player with the lowest total score is the winner.

CHAPTER 12

Introduction to Competitive Archery

AS WE END OUR ARCHERY JOURNEY TOGETHER, it is likely you still feel much more like a beginner than a world-class marksman. So, you may wonder, why devote the final chapter to the subject of competitive archery?

I have two good reasons. First, as a new archer, it is my hope you will also become a fan of the sport. And just as with any other sport, understanding the rules of the game and the various strategies involved are critical to fully appreciating the game. In American society, even casual sports fans absorb a fairly good understanding of popular ball sports such as baseball, football, basketball, and soccer through regular exposure. But if you approach the average sports fan on the street and ask about the format of Olympic archery competition, or how many points are awarded for a perfect shot on a 3-D target course, you are almost certain to be met with a blank stare! With that in mind, I want to spend the first part of this chapter providing a brief overview of today's most popular forms of archery competition.

Second, and perhaps more importantly, it is my hope you will see participation in some form of competitive archery as part of your natural progression as an archer. I realize you may not yet possess a lot of confidence in your shooting abilities. You also may not be an overly competitive person. On the other hand, it is possible you are already itching for the chance to test your mettle in the heat of battle! Either way, participating in "competitive" archery programs such as the National Archery in Schools Program, USA Archery's Junior Olympic Archery Development program, Scholastic 3-D Archery, or even a summer shooting league at your local pro shop will pay great dividends.

"Archery is a sport that requires a lot of repetitive training. Goal setting is an incredibly powerful tool in improving and measuring progress." said competitive recurve shooter Sarah Boyd, a 2015 Columbia University graduate who earned All-America honors and helped lead Columbia to the 2015 National Outdoor Collegiate Archery Championship.

Scoring your arrows is a great way to track your progress as a shooter because, regardless of where you start, you can set a goal to shoot progressively better scores. And while your score certainly provides a useful benchmark for your shooting, all the archery programs discussed here place as much emphasis on creating a positive atmosphere where shooters can not only improve their skills but also develop new friendships with fellow archers. As I have stressed throughout this book, archery is a diverse community of people held together by a common love of shooting, and finding your place in that community is one of the most rewarding aspects of being an archer. That's why I'll conclude this chapter with an overview of archery's top competitive development programs and information about how you can get involved.

OLYMPIC ARCHERY

Although there many types of archery competition, none gets more worldwide attention than the one held every four years at the Summer Olympics, where the world's top recurve shooters gather for the chance to earn a coveted gold medal—and the personal and national bragging rights that come with it.

Olympic archery competition is divided into five events: individual and team men's and women's competitions and, new for the Tokyo 2020 Games, a mixed-team competition. Regardless of the event, all Olympic archery competition is conducted outdoors. Archers use recurve bows that are part of the recurve division of World Archery, the sport's international federation. Olympic bows may have mechanical sights and stabilizers, but optical enhancements such as magnified scopes are prohibited. Olympic archery is conducted at a range of 70 meters (76.6 yards) using a target that is 122 centimeters (4 feet) in diameter. At 70 meters, the target face appears roughly the size of a thumbtack head held at arm's length. And Olympic competitors have to shoot at that target in all kinds of weather conditions, including rain and significant winds!

The target face features five colored rings, starting with gold in the center followed by red, blue, black, and white. Each colored ring measures about 2.5 inches wide and is further divided in half for a total of ten scoring zones, as follows:

Inner gold: 10 points (An even smaller circle inside the 10-ring is marked with a small "x" and is commonly called the "x-ring." Although

Olympic archery target PHOTO COURTESY OF MAPLE LEAF PRESS

still awarded 10 points, the number of shots placed in the x-ring is often used as a tiebreaker in competition.)

Outer gold: 9 points

Inner red: 8 points

Outer red: 7 points

Inner blue: 6 points

Outer blue: 5 points

Inner black: 4 points

Outer black: 3 points

Inner white: 2 points

Outer white: 1 point

Individual Competition

Individual Olympic archery competition features the top sixty-four male and female qualifiers from around the world, who face off in a head-to-head, match-play format to determine overall winners.

Initially, each shooter participates in a "Qualification round," with scores used to determine overall rankings from 1 to 64. Once the rankings are determined, competition moves into a bracket-style, match-play format, with top-ranked shooters facing the lowest ranked shooters (1 versus 64, 2 versus 63, etc.) and the winner of each match advancing to the next round.

Each head-to-head match is scored using a set system similar to that used in tennis, with a maximum of five sets. In each set, each archer shoots three arrows, with the archers alternating shots and each shooter having 20 seconds to shoot each arrow. For the first set, the higher ranked archer chooses who shoots first. In subsequent rounds, the trailing archer shoots first.

The combined score of all three arrows for each archer is his or her score for that set. An archer who wins a set receives 2 points; if the archers tie in a set, each shooter gets 1 point. If the archers are still tied 5–5 after five sets, the match is decided by a one-arrow shoot-off. In a tiebreaker, the archer who shot first in the first set goes first. If both archers shoot a 10, they shoot again. If not, the archer with the highest scoring arrow

MORE THAN AN OLYMPIC SPORT

Although the Olympic Games may get the lion's share of the attention due to the games' high profile, international archery competitions occur regularly, usually on an annual basis. And while only recurve bows are allowed in Olympic competition, most other events offer divisions for both recurve and compound shooters.

IMAGE COURTESY OF WORLD ARCHERY

International target archery events, including the Olympics, are sanctioned by World Archery, the sport's international federation. World Archery also runs a series of World Cup events each year and World Championships in various disciplines that are held every other year. In target archery, both indoor and outdoor recurve and compound events are held. Indoor competitions are shot at a range of 18 meters, while outdoor competitions are shot at distances up to 90 meters. More information about these events, as well as world archer rankings based on results from World Archery events, is available online at worldarchery.org.

is declared the winner, 6–5. If both arrows are the same score, then the archer whose arrow is closest to the center is declared the winner, 6–5.

Team Competition

The Olympic archery team competition typically consists of sixteen top teams from around the world, though the number can sometimes be smaller, depending on the outcome of qualifying competitions. Men's and women's Olympic archery teams have three shooters, while a mixed team features two shooters—one man and one woman.

As with individual competition, the initial stage of team archery is a ranking round, which determines the initial match-ups for the head-to-head competition that follows. If there are fewer than sixteen teams in the event, then top teams from the ranking round receive byes (automatic advancement to the next round) to even out the bracket.

Team competition is also scored using sets like the individual competition. However, in the team event, the first team to reach 5 points is declared the winner. Also, each team shoots four sets per match, with six total arrows (two by each shooter) shot in each set. Each team has a total of 2 minutes for its three archers to shoot their two shots each; after all

From left, 2016 US men's Olympic archery team members Zach Garrett, Brady Ellison, and Jake Kaminski captured the silver medal in Rio de Janeiro, Brazil. Ellison also captured the bronze medal in the men's individual archery competition. PHOTO COURTESY OF BRADY ELLISON

shots are fired, the team with the highest total score is the winner of that set. Winning a set is worth 2 points; if the teams tie in a set, each team gets 1 point.

If the teams are still tied after four sets, each archer shoots one arrow in a shoot-off; the team with the highest total score is declared the winner. If the teams are still tied after the shoot-off, the victory goes to the team with the single arrow closest to the center of the target.

3-D ARCHERY

Another very popular form of bow and arrow competition is 3-D archery, which involves shooting a series of life-size foam animal targets. Although some 3-D competitions are held indoors, most of the time targets are set on a roving, outdoor wooded course designed to simulate realistic bowhunting scenarios. There are thousands of archery clubs nationwide that host recreational 3-D shoots, but the biggest events in the 3-D world are conducted by two organizations: the Archery Shooters Association (asaarchery.com) and International Bowhunting Organization (www.ibo.net). ASA and IBO events are open to both professional and amateur archers who compete for cash prizes in a variety of shooting classes encompassing all types of archery gear, from modern compounds to traditional longbows. ASA president Mike Tyrell said more than 4,000

3-D archery shoots are a great activity for all ages and genders. PHOTO COURTESY OF THE ARCHERY TRADE ASSOCIATION

shooters of all ages and ability levels participate in the organization's six major events each year.

"Probably 30 percent of all participants at ASA events are either moms or kids, so it's truly a family event," Tyrell said.

Although the number of targets shot and scoring system can vary slightly from competition to competition, the overall goal in 3-D archery is to place arrows in the "vital area" of the foam animal targets, with points being awarded based on accuracy. In an official ASA competition, for example, the event consists of two rounds of twenty targets each. Top shooters compete on "unknown distance" courses, where range estimation up to 50 yards is part of the game; novices can shoot "known distance" courses, where the distance to each target is clearly marked. In both cases, competitors get one shot at each target, with points awarded depending on the point of impact. In ASA events, the best possible shot is a 12, which is achieved by hitting one of two 1.75-inch-diameter 12-rings on the target. Ten points are awarded for hitting a 5-inch-diameter 10-ring, 8 points for hitting a larger 8-ring that covers the animal's entire vital area, and 5 points for hitting anywhere else on the target. Misses, as you might expect, are awarded 0 points. ASA targets also have a special 14-ring in the upper rear of the 8-ring that is reserved for special bonus competition.

This Delta-McKenzie Killzone target shows the various scoring rings used for ASA and IBO 3-D tournaments. PHOTO COURTESY OF DMT TARGETS

To put the 3-D scoring system into perspective, Tyrell used a golf analogy, explaining that a 10 is basically a par, while a 12 is a birdie. An 8 is similar to a bogey, and a 5 is essentially a double bogey. Deciding whether to shoot for one of the 12-rings instead of the larger 10-ring involves a lot of strategy, Tyrell noted.

"If you misjudge the distance, you could fall out to an 8 or even a 5, so it's kind of a risk/reward shot," he said.

Although the size of various animal targets used in 3-D archery varies greatly—all the way from small critters such as raccoons and coyotes to life-size elk or bison, even dinosaurs—Tyrell explained that the size of the scoring rings is the same on every target. He also noted that ASA imposes

PROFESSIONAL ARCHERS?

Professional archers may not make as much money or be as famous as their counterparts in football, baseball, basketball, or hockey, but the world's top shots can still earn a very good living off their shooting skills.

Cash prizes in the professional divisions of top archery competitions regularly run in the thousands of dollars. The biggest and most prestigious archery competition of the year is the World Archery Festival—more commonly known as The Vegas Shoot—held each winter in Las Vegas, Nevada. In 2016 The Vegas Shoot attracted more than 3,000 competitors from around the world, with more than $300,000 in prize money awarded. Italian compound bow archer Sergio Pagni cashed a record $45,000 check for his win in the Freestyle Championship Male division, while US Olympian Brady Ellison pocketed a cool $10,000 for his win in the Recurve Championship Male division.

Professional archer Levi Morgan shows off his contingency check from Mathews, his bow sponsor, after winning the ASA's Pro/Am Tournament in London, Kentucky, in June 2018. For top shooters such as Morgan, a ten-time ASA Shooter of the Year and multiple world champion, bonus money paid by sponsors for top tournament finishes far exceeds actual tournament winnings. PHOTO COURTESY OF LEVI MORGAN

In addition to the actual prize money awarded by tournament organizers, top professional archers also have the opportunity to earn "contingency" money from their sponsors. Bow manufacturers and other companies that make arrows, bow sights, release aids, and other gear offer payouts to sponsored archers who win or place near the top of the standings. In essence, contingency payouts reward successful archers for demonstrating the quality and accuracy of the equipment they use in competition. And in many cases, the amount an archer makes from sponsor contingencies is more than the actual tournament prize money. For example, it was estimated that the total value of Pagni's win at The Vegas Shoot in 2016 was more than $100,000 when factoring in contingency payouts—not a bad paycheck for three days' work!

an arrow speed limit of 290 feet per second for pro classes and 280 feet per second for amateur classes to prevent bigger, stronger archers from gaining an unfair advantage as a result of the flatter arrow trajectory faster arrows have.

"The arrow speed rule is really designed to level the playing field, the same way restrictor plates do in NASCAR," Tyrell said.

FIELD ARCHERY

The final type of archery competition I want to discuss is field archery, which combines elements of both traditional target shooting and 3-D shooting into a unique format that offers a good variety of action. Major field archery events are sanctioned by the National Field Archery Association (nfaausa .com), which hosts numerous state, sectional, and national events annually.

Although the format of competition can vary at the local club level, a traditional field archery event consists of three disciplines—a field round, a hunter round, and an animal round—with archers vying to compile the highest overall score. National NFAA events are typically conducted over several days, with competitors completing one discipline each day.

Archers compete in the 2018 NFAA Nationals in Mechanicsburg, Pennsylvania.
PHOTO COURTESY OF JEFF SANCHEZ/BOWDOC ARCHERY

NFAA field target PHOTO COURTESY OF MAPLE LEAF PRESS

In the field round, competitors shoot two rounds of fourteen targets at distances of 15 to 80 yards. Four arrows are shot at each target, which vary in size depending on the distance of the shot. The official NFAA field target has a black center, followed by two white rings and two outer black rings. The inner black is worth 5 points, the white rings worth 4 points, and the outer black rings worth 3 points.

In the hunter round, competitors shoot two rounds of fourteen targets at distances of 11 to 70 yards. As with the field round, four arrows are shot at each target, which varies slightly from the field target. The NFAA hunter target is all black, with a white center bull's-eye and two outer black rings. The center white area is worth 5 points, the first black ring worth 4 points, and the outer black ring worth 3 points.

Finally, in the animal round, competitors shoot two rounds of fourteen targets at distances from 10 to 60 yards. Smaller animals are used for shorter shots, while larger animal targets are used at longer ranges. Each

NFAA hunter target PHOTO COURTESY OF MAPLE LEAF PRESS

NFAA animal target PHOTO COURTESY OF MAPLE LEAF PRESS

WHERE TO WATCH ARCHERY COMPETITIONS

Outside the Olympics, you aren't likely to see archery competition on major network television. However, that doesn't mean there aren't plenty of opportunities to watch world-class shooters in action. The following online resources are good places to start if you're interested in viewing a sampling of archery competition:

There are a number of ways to follow top archery competitions online, including World Archery's YouTube channel, which includes live and archived coverage from major tournaments. Here, US archer Mackenzie Brown competes in a tournament in Mexico in 2017. PHOTO COURTESY OF WORLD ARCHERY

Archery TV (youtube.com/user/archerytv): World Archery's YouTube channel features highlights from top events, athlete interviews, fan videos, and more.

USA Archery TV (youtube.com/user/USAArcheryTV): USA Archery's YouTube channel features news and highlights from the national team and other USA Archery events around the country.

Lancaster Archery Classic (lancasterarchery.com/archery-classic/): Lancaster Archery in Lancaster, Pennsylvania, hosts a large indoor tournament each winter that attracts hundreds of top shooters from around the world. In addition to producing its own live, online broadcast during the tournament, you can watch footage from past events.

Bow Junky (bowjunky.com): This popular, archery-only website is geared toward die-hard archery addicts and includes links to scores of videos of top competitions from across the nation.

animal target has two scoring zones—a smaller, oblong zone corresponding to the vital area of the animal, and a larger zone roughly corresponding to the outline of the animal's body. Inside the smaller zone on each target is a small "bonus dot" that scores a 1-point bonus. In the animal round, archers may shoot a maximum of three arrows at each target, with only the highest-scoring arrow counted. A maximum of 21 points per target can be earned, depending on the location of the hit and whether it was the first, second, or third arrow. For example, hitting the small bonus dot on the first arrow yields 21 points; hitting the bonus dot with the second or third arrows yields 17 and 13 points, respectively.

As in target and 3-D archery, NFAA events offer a variety of competition classes depending on an archer's skill level and type of archery equipment used. NFAA also uses a national handicapping system, similar to that used in golf, to allow archers of varying ability levels to compete on a level basis.

BECOMING A COMPETITOR

As a new shooter, there are many great opportunities available for trying your hand at archery competition. Whether you are simply interested in the experience or have your heart set on being a champion, the programs discussed below will help you learn the ropes and likely make some new friends along the way.

National Archery in the Schools Program (naspschools.com): Founded in Kentucky in 2002, NASP quickly spread across the nation and helps introduce more than 2.2 million school-age children to archery each year. The NASP curriculum is based on national educational standards and designed to be implemented as part of a school's regular physical education program. NASP uses "universal fit" Genesis compound bows that have no let-off or set draw length, so they can be shared among students. To keep things as simple as possible, the NASP program does not use bow sights or mechanical release aids, instead focusing on the fundamentals of archery and instinctive shooting. School teams and individual archers have the opportunity to participate in state- and national-level NASP competitions. In 2016 the NASP National Tournament in Kentucky attracted a record-breaking 14,000 student archers from across the nation. Also in 2016, NASP launched a new Academic Archer program to further motivate and recognize high academic performance among program participants.

The NASP program has introduced millions of school-age children to archery since its inception in 2002. NASP uses "universal fit" Genesis compound bows that can be shared among students, making the sport accessible to children of all sizes. PHOTO COURTESY OF NATIONAL ARCHERY IN SCHOOLS PROGRAM

USA Archery Junior Olympic Archery Development Clubs (teamusa.org/youth): Open to all archers ages 8 to 20, JOAD is a USA Archery program designed to teach the fundamentals of archery in a fun, exciting environment that recognizes student achievement and prepares them for competition.

JOAD offers recurve, compound, and barebow archers the opportunity to learn range safety and proper shooting technique in an environment that also fosters focus, increased self-confidence, and team-building skills. Although introductory JOAD classes focus on fundamentals, there are intermediate and advanced JOAD classes where more experienced shooters can continue developing their skills. Many of America's top archers in international competition are graduates of the JOAD program.

JOAD classes are taught by certified instructors at USA Archery member clubs nationwide. Visit the JOAD website to locate a class in your area.

USA Archery Adult Archery Program (teamusa.org/usa-archery/archers/adult-archery-program): Similar to the JOAD program, USA

Although many introductory archery programs are focused on youth, a number of programs are focused on new adult shooters, including USA Archery's Adult Archery Program, which teaches archery fundamentals to those ages 21 and older. PHOTO COURTESY OF THE ARCHERY TRADE ASSOCIATION

Archery's Adult Archery Program is designed to teach the fundamentals of archery to adults age 21 and over. The program will also prepare participants for competition, if they so desire. Participation provides the opportunity to make new friends, a great upper-body workout, and the chance to build self-confidence and learn team-building skills. Like JOAD, Adult Archery Programs are taught by certified instructors at clubs nationwide. Visit the USA Archery website to locate a program in your area.

Scholastic 3-D Archery Association (s3da.org): Founded in 2012, Scholastic 3-D Archery is an after-school youth program designed to build upon the success of NASP and other entry-level archery programs. S3DA programs can be affiliated with schools, archery clubs, or archery retailers. S3DA students focus on improving their shooting skills and participating in local, state, and national 3-D target competitions based on the format of the Archery Shooters Association (ASA). Other S3DA partners include USA Archery, the National Field Archery Association (NFAA), and the Pope and Young Club, a national bowhunting and conservation organization.

The Scholastic 3-D Archery Association is an after-school program that focuses on helping young archers improve their skills and give them opportunities to compete in local, state, and national 3-D target competitions. PHOTO COURTESY OF THE SCHOLASTIC 3-D ARCHERY ASSOCIATION

Local archery leagues (archery360.com): In addition to the specific programs mentioned here, many archery clubs and retail shops across the nation offer informal, weekly archery leagues that provide an opportunity to learn more about the sport while developing new friendships and engaging in some friendly competition. There are a wide variety of leagues geared toward youth, adults, and families. The Archery Trade Association's Archery 360 website has a finder tool to locate archery clubs, pro shops, and instructors in your area.

INDEX

accessories/related gear, 24–37, 53
accuracy problems. *See* trouble-
    shooting
aiming
    about, 74–75
    aiming dot, floating, 76
    bow sight, adjusting, 77–80
    as mind-set, 101–4
    practical application, 104–5
aluminum arrows, 24, 58
anchoring, 73–74, 97–99, 122
Archery Shooters Association,
    148–49, 151
Archery 360 website, 6
Archery Trade Association, 6
Archery TV, 154
arm guards, 34, 64
arrow rests, 27
arrows
    about, 22–24
    inspecting, 58–59
    nocking, 59, 68–69
    retrieving, 60, 62
axle-to-axle length, 50

back tension. *See also* surprise
    release
    defined, 107–8
    exercise for, 109
    importance of, 116–17
    release aids, 114–15
bag targets, 37
Balloon Explosion (game), 133–35
Baseball (game), 140–41
binoculars, 36
Blackjack (game), 137–38
bone-on-bone anchor reference,
    97–99

Bow Junky, 154
bow length, 48–50
Bowling (game), 130–31
bow-mounted quivers, 33
bows. *See also specific bow types*
    adjustability/shareability, 51–53
    bow length, 48–50
    bow weight, 50–51
    cool factor, 45
    damaged/worn, 57–58, 121
    draw length, 43–44, 46–48
    draw weight, 46–48
    equipment, additional, 53
    eye dominance and, 42
    pointing in safe direction, 60, 61
    trying before buying, 43
    for women, 49
    for youths, 49, 51–52
bow sights, 25, 77–80
bow slings, 29
bow stands, 34
bow stringers, 32
bow torque, 86, 87, 124–25
bow weight, 50–51
Boyd, Sarah, 143–44
Brown, Mackenzie, 154

cam systems, 21
carbon arrows, 24, 58–59
chest protectors, 35
clickers, 32, 113, 116
competitive archery
    about, 143–44
    field archery, 151–53, 155
    Olympic archery, 144–48
    professional archers, 150
    programs, 155–58
    3-D archery, 148–49, 151

watching online, 154
compound bows
    about, 8–10, 20–21
    adjustability/shareability, 51–53
    aiming, 75, 104
    anchoring, 73–74, 97, 99
    back tension, 107, 115
    bow length, 50
    drawing, 95–96
    draw length, 44, 47–48
    equipment, additional, 22, 53
    limitations, 22
    mechanics, 21–22
    parts, 20
    releasing, 81
    surprise release, 110–12
    uses, 22

Darts (game), 139–40
dealers, archery, 6, 41, 43, 53
drawing and anchoring sequence
    anchoring, 97–99
    drawing the bow, 73, 94–97
    pre-draw, 91–94
draw length, 43–44, 46–48, 50
draw weight, 46–48
Dudley, John, 91, 101–2, 109
dynamic pull, 107–8

Ellison, Brady, 4, 8, 147, 150
equipment problems, 57–59,
    119–21
Explore Archery programs, 132
eye dominance, 42

facial pressure, 122–24
feathers, orienting, 68–69
field archery, 151–53, 155
Find It (game), 137
flaws, shooting. See trouble-
    shooting
fletching, 24
flinching, 127–28
Follow the Arrow (game), 132–33

follow-through, 82, 126–28
Four in a Row (game), 136

games, archery
    Balloon Explosion, 133–35
    Baseball, 140–41
    Blackjack, 137–38
    Bowling, 130–31
    Darts, 139–40
    Find It, 137
    Follow the Arrow, 132–33
    Four in a Row, 136
    Golf, 140, 141, 142
    Horseshoes, 131–32
    Inside the Rings, 133
    Poker, 137–38
    Split the Arrow, 136–37
    Tic-Tac-Toe, 135–36
Garrett, Zach, 147
Genesis bows, 52–53, 155, 156
gloves, shooting, 30
goals, setting, 10–11
Golf (game), 140, 141, 142
grip, 70–71, 91, 124
guards, arm, 34, 64

head position, 95–97
hip quivers, 33
history of archery, 2–3
Horseshoes (game), 131–32
house rules, 62

injuries, 57
Inside the Rings (game), 133
International Bowhunting
    Organization, 148, 149
International Limb Fitting
    system, 18

Kaminski, Jake, 147
kisser buttons, 26, 99

Lancaster Archery Classic, 154
laser rangefinders, 36–37
layered foam targets, 38

leagues, local, 158
longbows
    about, 10, 13, 14
    aiming, 74
    bow length, 48–50
    draw length, 44, 46–47
    equipment, additional, 15
    limitations, 14–15
    mechanics, 14
    parts, 13
    uses, 14

Morgan, Levi, 150
multi-pin sights, 79–80, 104

National Archery in the Schools
        Program, 52, 53, 57,
        155–56
National Field Archery
        Association, 151–53, 155
neutral stance, 65–67, 87–88
nock fit, 68, 69
nocking arrows, 59, 68–69
nocking loops, 28
nock sets, 27
nocks, 24
nock wrenches, 69

Olympic archery
    about, 19, 144–45
    individual competition, 145–47
    Rio (2016), 3, 4
    team competition, 147–48
Olympic recurve bows. *See also*
        traditional recurve bows
    about, 8, 17–18
    aiming, 75, 104–5
    anchoring, 73, 97, 99
    drawing, 95, 97
    equipment, additional, 19
    limitations, 19
    mechanics, 18–19
    parts, 18
    releasing, 81

surprise release, 112–13, 116
    uses, 19
open stance, 88–89

Pagni, Sergio, 150
parents, 6–7, 55, 83–84
"peeking," 82, 127
peep sights, 25–26, 104
Pfeil, Heather, 7
plucked string, 125
points, 24
Poker (game), 137–38
popularity of archery, 3–4
pre-draw, 91–94
preloading, 86, 87
professional archers, 150

quivers, 33

rangefinders, laser, 36–37
recreational bows, 7
recurve bows. *See* Olympic
        recurve bows; traditional
        recurve bows
release, 81, 110–13, 116, 126–27
release aids, 31, 81, 110–12,
        114–15
release hand, 71
rests, arrow, 27
rhythm, finding, 83–84
rules, safety, 57–62
running with archery gear, 60

safety
    importance of, 55–57
    injuries, 57
    parents, note to, 55
    rules, 57–62
    whistle commands, archery
        range, 56
Scholastic 3-D Archery
        Association, 157–58
screws, loose, 119–21
shafts, 24

shooting gloves, 30
shooting tabs, 30–31
shops, archery, 6, 41, 43, 53
shot, time for making, 83
shot distance, initial, 63, 65
sight pins, 102–4
single sights, 79
slings, bow, 29
solid foam targets, 38
Split the Arrow (game), 136–37
square stance, 89
stabilizers, 28–29
stance
   about, 85–87
   finding, 65–67
   ideal, 89
   inconsistent, 122
   neutral, 65–67, 87–88
   open, 88–89
   square, 89
stands, bow, 34
static pull, 107, 108
stringers, bow, 32
surprise release, 110–13, 116. See
   also back tension

tabs, shooting, 30–31
target panic, 116–17
targets, 37–38, 60, 61, 149
tension-activated back-tension
   release aids, 114–15
T form, 72, 73, 94–95
3-D archery, 148–49, 151, 157–58
Tic-Tac-Toe (game), 135–36
traditional recurve bows. See also
   Olympic recurve bows
   about, 10, 15
   adjustability/shareability, 51
   aiming, 74
   anchoring, 73, 97
   back tension, 107

bow length, 48–50
draw length, 44, 46–47
equipment, additional, 17, 53
limitations, 17
mechanics, 16
parts, 15
pre-draw, 94
releasing, 81
uses, 16–17
troubleshooting
   anchor, inconsistent, 122
   bow torque, 124–25
   equipment problems, 119–21
   facial pressure, 122–24
   follow-through, poor, 126–28
   grip, poor, 124
   plucked string, 125
   stance, inconsistent, 122
Tyrell, Mike, 148–49, 151

Ulmer, Randy, 85–87
USA Archery Adult Archery
   Program, 156–57
USA Archery Junior Olympic
   Archery Development
   Clubs, 156
USA Archery TV, 154

vanes/feathers, orienting, 68–69
Vegas Shoot, The, 150

walk-back tuning, 80
whistle commands, archery
   range, 56
women archers, 49
World Archery, 146
World Archery Festival, 150
wrenches, nock, 69

youth archers, 49, 51–52. See also
   National Archery in the
   Schools Program